ING

Big Horn Mtns

o Hole in the wall

CASPER

NORTH PLATTE RIVER

Oregon Trail

SWEETWATER RIVER

RAWLINS

N. PLATTE RIVER

Ft Laramie

H PASS

RED DESERET

o FT STEELE

LARAMIE

CHEYENNE

U.P. RR

laCLEDE STAGE STATION

BRIDGER'S PASS

80

RADO

Overland

Booms and Busts
on Bitter Creek

Booms & Busts on Bitter Creek

A HISTORY OF ROCK SPRINGS, WYOMING

By
Robert B. Rhode

Robert B. Rhode
June 1, 1987

PRUETT **P** *PUBLISHING COMPANY*
Boulder, Colorado

First Edition

1 2 3 4 5 6 7 8 9

Printed in the United States of America.

Library of Congress Cataloging-in-Publication Data

Rhode, Robert Bartlett, 1916-
   Booms and busts on Bitter Creek.

   Bibliography: p.
   Includes index.
   1. Rock Springs (Wyo.)—History. I. Title.
F769.R6R46   1986   978.7'85   86-22714
ISBN 0-87108-719-7

To
Rena

Contents

Contents

Preface

The story of Rock Springs is in large part a microcosm of the story of the United States with, of course, significant peculiarities largely due to the environment on Bitter Creek and the heavy influence of the Union Pacific Railroad and its coal company.

This is a short narrative history of Rock Springs and its people designed for the general reader. The choices about what to include and the unavoidable and painful choices about what to omit have been made by the author. I tried to provide as clear and accurate an account as possible within limited space, with some detail on individual stories that seemed to provide insight into the story of the community and its people.

I am indebted to a great many, especially my wife, Rena. The preparation of this book was particularly rewarding for both of us because of the generous way in which so many have shared their experiences and ideas or offered support in other ways. They include members of the Fedrizzi family: our nephew David, brothers Livio (Rat) and Guido, and sister-in-law Louise. Also we must acknowledge very special help in a variety of ways from Art Rosatti, Lewis Zaversnik, Mr. and Mrs. John W. Hay, Jr., Robert H. Johnson, Edwin James, William R. Dickson, Mary Dickson, Mr. and Mrs. John L. (Grouch) Taucher, Rudolph (Rudy) Anselmi, Elmer Halseth, Tom Manatos, Sylvia Pulos, Gwen Ainscough, Ann Dominiske, Helen Pulos, Paul Wataha, and the late Vernon O. Murray, whom we were able to interview before his death and who offered us use of a number of printed sources from his personal files.

It was after our first visit to the Sweetwater County Historical Museum in Green River and a chat with the director, Henry Chadey, and his assistant, Mae Wright, that we decided to attempt this work. The generous sharing of their knowledge of sources and the museum's rich collection of materials we were freely permitted to use were vital to this project, and we are deeply grateful. Help in finding other printed sources came from various members of the staff of Norlin Library, University of Colorado, Boulder, especially persons in the Western History Collection, Interlibrary Loan Office, and the Government Documents Division. We also are in debt to Jean Brainerd and Roger Joyce at the Historical Research and Publications Division of the Wyoming Archives, Museums, and Historical Department in Cheyenne for their help, and to Jean Thompson and others at the Rock Springs Public Library.

All of the above and more deserve a share in whatever credit is due, but none bear any share of blame for errors, interpretations, or omissions. Those are the author's responsibility.

Robert B. Rhode
Boulder, Colorado

1

The Lonesome Land

Sun-baked and treeless, the valley of the Bitter Creek offered no shady rest stops for the U.S. Army survey party returning to "the States" in 1850 after a year in the Great Salt Lake Valley. The nineteen men, with mounts and pack mules, had expected nothing of Bitter Creek except a way east to the Continental Divide, until they stopped to stare at a black streak, several feet deep, across the face of the sandstone bluff above them. This clear sign of rich coal deposits gave the creek's barren valley a new significance.

Commanding this group was Howard Stansbury, a captain in the United States Army. For this day he noted in his journal, "We found a bed of bituminous coal cropping out of the north bluff of the valley, with every indication of its being quite abundant." This outcrop of coal was evidently on a bluff above what is now known as West Flat in the town of Rock Springs, Wyoming. The next day, in his journal entry for September 16, he wrote that they had found evidence of a number of other coal seams as they followed Bitter Creek eastward. Stansbury's report of this expedition, published in various editions, became something of a best seller for its day. In it he wrote that the coal along Bitter Creek seemed to exist in "quantities apparently without limit." That observation proved to be most interesting and persuasive a few years later as other men planned a route for a transcontinental railroad.

Stansbury's ancestors had settled in the American colonies before the Revolutionary War. His grandfather, Joseph Stansbury, was a British Loyalist who had carried messages between the Revolutionary War traitor Benedict Arnold and the British army commanders, and as a consequence he found he was more comfortable living in England after the war. His descendants, however, including his grandson Howard, were accepted as loyal Americans. Howard, a civil engineer, was forty-four years old in the year that he explored the Bitter Creek Valley and in his twelfth year with the U.S. Army topographic engineers. He had been placed in charge of an expedition that left Fort Leavenworth, Kansas, in the spring of 1949, with orders to survey the area around the Great Salt Lake in the region that was to become the Utah Territory. His survey party completed its task during the summer of 1950 and on August 28 started back for "the states." A week later they rode "over the rim" of the Bear River Divide at the western boundary of today's state of Wyoming. Ahead lay a comparatively easy trek down gentle slopes into the vast Green River Basin, and to the already famous, if shabby, Fort Bridger, on the Black's Fork of the Green River.

Jim Bridger's fort was a temporary haven for the tide of migrants headed for the Far West in trains of covered wagons. The sight of Fort Bridger was especially welcome for the migrants because it meant they had survived a frustratingly expansive barrier, the high and vast lonesome land later to be called Wyoming. The first wave of wagon trains came by Fort Bridger from 1842 through 1845; they were home seekers headed for the reputed abundance of the Columbia River country in Oregon. That migration was followed by the great trek of the Mormons, seeking religious freedom in 1847, and then by those rushing to California seeking gold in 1849 and 1850.

When he arrived at the fort Stansbury sought out Jim Bridger, veteran mountain man and scout, for a talk about the next lap of his trip east. If he continued on the much-used Oregon-California Trail it meant added time and miles on a wide northward arc to cross the Continental Divide at South Pass and then a swing back to the southeast along the North Platte River to Fort Laramie. Stansbury hoped a direct route, preferably straight east, was possible.

Bridger was only two years older than Stansbury, but twenty-five years more experienced in the trails of the Rocky Mountain West. In 1822 when he was eighteen, Bridger had gone up the Missouri River with a fur-gathering expedition sponsored by

William Ashley. He had been absent from the mountain west for only brief periods since. By 1850 he was one of the most celebrated and picturesque characters of the frontier, and one of the most knowledgeable. Sure, he knew of a more direct route back to the states, and he would act as guide.

They left the squalid fort that squatted between two channels of the Black's Fork River on September 10, 1850, following the rutted migrant road for the first two days. "Clouds of dust at every turn of the road announced the approach of crowds of emigrant wagons" headed west, Stansbury wrote in his journal.

On September 12 Jim Bridger must have stopped the Stansbury party to point to the outline of a large mesa, isolated by its hugeness and by the immensity of space around it, jutting up from the barren land some forty miles to the east. This was Pilot Butte, a remnant of what was once an ocean of lava from a volcanic eruption. It had been used as a landmark by Bridger and the other mountain men who traveled about the Green River Basin for twenty years beginning in 1812, and evidently named by them.

Bridger turned off the migrant trail, which continued to the northeast, and led Stansbury's party directly east, toward the butte. Stansbury looked ahead and saw only "dreary desolation, saddening to the heart." In his journal he also wrote: "The whole country looks as if it had, at one time, been the bottom of a vast lake." He was right. Geologists have since determined that this large basin of the Green River in present-day Wyoming was at one prehistoric time covered by a great inland sea.

On the map prepared by the cartographers with Stansbury the area that extends from a few miles east of Fort Bridger to approximately the present location of the town of Rawlins was labeled as "Artemisia Barrens with some pasture on the water courses." The genus of plants known as *Artemisia* includes the sagebrush, that amazingly hardy plant that appears, at casual glance, to be the only thing growing on these high plains and hills. Travelers new to this area generally believe there is one other thing that helps sagebrush fill this seemingly endless wilderness of space—the wind.

Bridger led the survey team along the Black's Fork River

toward the dominating stream of the area, the mighty Green, then sometimes called by one of its Indian names, *Seeds-ke-dee* or *Sisk-ke-de* (prairie hen). For campfires at night they used mostly sagebrush; it made a quick hot fire, and there was seldom anything else available. At the point where Black's Fork turns sharply south before it joins the Green, the riders, still leading their pack mules, followed Bridger east over a ridge and down a long, winding ravine called Rabbit Hollow to the Green, which they found in its usual autumn mood—placid, only about three feet deep, but with thirty-foot banks eight hundred feet apart. They forded, then turned downstream for about two miles to the point where Bitter Creek, coming from the east, empties its alkali-laden water into the Green.

Previously, Indians—Shoshoni from the north and Utes from the south—had visited this land occasionally when it was favored by the buffalo. The valley that the wind, the rain, and the creek had carved, leaving sandy hills and rocky bluffs here and there, provided a winter haven for the shaggy herds because it was relatively free of deep snow. But by 1850 the buffalo no longer came to the Bitter Creek Valley.

William Ashley, early entrepreneur in the fur trade, had led a group of men across the valley in 1825 seeking beaver to trap; they found nothing to keep them or bring them back. Twenty-four years later a party of Cherokee Indians from Arkansas, who had joined the rush for the California goldfields, blazed a route west across the hills south of Bitter Creek in 1849, but this Cherokee Trail attracted only a small minority of travelers in the next decade.

Scarcity of potable water was a major factor in the unpopularity of this region. The water of Bitter Creek, aptly named, is so sour with alkali dissolved from the land that humans drink it only in desperation, and most beasts will accept it only on those terms as well. Here in 1850 was a sort of no man's land, or at least a valley not particularly coveted by any man—until the white man found the coal beds.

It was near the end of their first day of travel along Bitter Creek that the Stansbury party saw their first coal outcrop. After leaving the area of the coal seams they continued along Bitter Creek, sighting several bands of antelope, abundant numbers of grouse, and one bear. To continue east they had to leave Bitter Creek where it curves south, and from that point their route had a more noticeable upward slant. They were slowly climbing to the Continental Divide, which they crossed where a line of hills gives way to a slight depression. This was Bridger's Pass at an elevation of about seven thousand feet. In his report Stansbury called attention to "that remarkable depression" he thought was "hitherto unknown." However, it was the same divide crossing the Cherokees had used a year earlier. Stansbury thought the pass significant for a possible "post route," perhaps a railway, and for a way to reach those rich coal deposits along Bitter Creek. Motorists on today's Interstate 80 cross the Continental Divide about fifteen miles north of Bridger's Pass.

In less than one day's dusty travel down the eastern slope of the divide after crossing the pass, Stansbury reached a plentiful source of fresh, cool water in the North Platte River. Here the survey party was refreshed by waters that started out in the Medicine Bow Mountains near the Wyoming-Colorado border. From the point where Stansbury crossed going east, the North Platte flows on north for nearly fifty miles before it is joined by the Sweetwater River near the "register of the desert," Independence Rock, where thousands of migrants carved their names. The North Platte then curves east and finally southeast into Nebraska. In that stretch it was the stream the old Oregon-California Trail followed.

Early in October Stansbury was resting at Fort Laramie, his "reconnaissance of a New Route through the Rocky Mountains," as he called it, successfully completed. His report, first published in 1852 and reprinted several times, was popular reading, in England as well as the United States. Even so the westward migration continued to follow the longer northern route along the North Platte and over South Pass rather than using the shorter route over Bridger's Pass.

An early stagecoach line to the Far West, operated by Russell, Majors and Wardell, used the South Pass route as well, beginning in 1859. But that famous stageline partnership slipped into bankruptcy because of reckless investments made by one of the partners. The federal government, however, needed a carrier for the mails so it offered a subsidy to a replacement stageline over the same route. That line soon was acquired at public auction by the man who became known as the "king" of the stagecoach business in the Rocky Mountain West, a frontiersman turned entrepreneur, tough, rough, and canny Ben Holladay.

The swelling tide of whites along the migrant road fueled spreading anger among the Indians, especially the Sioux. The fragile peace between Indians and whites supposedly established by the Great Council at Fort Laramie in 1851 was shattered by a full-scale war beginning in 1862.

Raiding Indians often concentrated their efforts on stealing the fine, big horses kept at the relay stations for pulling the stagecoaches. Finally the raids virtually halted the stageline traffic, and the postmaster general began sending all mail for the West Coast by ship around the southern tip of South America. To save his Overland Stageline, Holladay on July 18, 1862, gave the order to move it south to the Cherokee Trail. New stage stations were built on a line running north from Denver, across the Laramie Plains, over Bridger's Pass, thence along Stansbury's route down Bitter Creek to the Green and on to Fort Bridger. When the rattling stages began running on the new route in August 1862, they brought to reality one of the developments. Stansbury had foreseen: the post route over Bridger's Pass. Because his line was called the Overland Stage, Holladay promoted the name Overland Trail for this Bridger's Pass route, and this has resulted in some confusion ever since because the older South Pass route was often referred to as the Overland.

Economics as well as Indian troubles dictated the switch to the more southern route. It made sense to send the main stageline southwest from North Platte, Nebraska, to follow the South Platte River to Julesburg, Colorado, and then on to Denver, because the Colorado gold rush, beginning in 1859, had created booming settlements in that area. Many of the wagon trains of freighters and migrants followed Holladay's lead.

The move south did not end the stageline's troubles with Indians. There were horse-stealing raids and a few bloody battles in 1863, and in 1864 a frightful and fiery renewal of warfare developed east of the Rocky Mountains from the plains of Nebraska through eastern Colorado to near Denver, and many lonely stage stations farther west, from Laramie to Bitter Creek, were also targets for Indian raids.

Another peace council at Fort Laramie in 1866 failed to halt the fighting, although most of the battles thereafter occurred a hundred miles or more north of the newly established Overland Trail. Holladay was able to reestablish regular stage service throughout the Overland route in 1865. His advertisements in Denver newspapers promised stage passengers they would be in Salt Lake City five days after departure from Denver; that would be at the rate of nearly one hundred miles every twenty-four hours. The stages traveled at an average speed of four to six miles an hour, through daylight and darkness, stopping every ten to twelve miles to change horses, and every forty to fifty miles for meals. Each stop was welcomed by the passengers for the temporary freedom from bruising jolts, choking dust, and painful cramps.

Wheeling over the alkali flats along Bitter Creek the most resplendent of the coaches might have seemed flamboyant abnormalities: red-painted bodies, yellow running gear, black trim, and western scenes painted on the door panels. But by the time any stagecoach reached the Bitter Creek area from either direction it was undoubtedly so coated with dust or mud that its original splendor was largely invisible. The teams for the coaches were matched horses or mules, all gray or black or brown.

Holladay employed seventy-five drivers, and each drove for fifty or sixty miles before he was relieved. Drivers were changed at the "home" stations, which had larger accommodations than the intermediate stops. At home stations meals could be served and sleeping bunks provided if needed. Some had blacksmith shops and other facilities for repairs. There was a home station where the present town of Green River is located.

Between the home stations were at least two, sometimes

three, "swing" stations, a name that came from the term used for the center pair of horses or mules in a team of six. The center pair was the swing pair. The stations were about twelve miles apart on the average, and the teams were changed at every station. Swing stations were lonely outposts, compared to the home stations, which became centers of such social activity as occurred in this region beyond the frontier line. Some home stations developed into crude wayside inns. The stock tender at the swing station, on the other hand, had to depend for social contact on the arrival of the stages twice each twenty-four hours, one from the east, one from the west. And the stages stayed only long enough for a change of teams. Other passersby included freighters, usually traveling in trains of several ox-drawn wagons, and migrants in groups of covered wagons.

Station tenders were usually rough, hermitic characters, and sometimes irascible fellows who sought little social contact. But some did their best to be hospitable whenever a guest appeared, although with the meager supplies at hand this hospitality was at best barely modest. One story, probably an invention, reported that a stock tender offered a temporary guest a noon meal in his log shelter. He sliced off and handed his guest a generous hunk of fat pork.

"No, thanks," said the guest. "I never eat that."

"Okay," replied the host. "Then help yourself to the mustard."

That anecdote, whether real or invented, quickly spread the length of the Overland Trail, and thereafter the usual response to any mention of the sparse amenities was, "Help yourself to the mustard."

From Waskie Station, the second west of the Continental Divide, to Almond Station at Point of Rocks on Bitter Creek, a distance of fifty miles, ran the part of the trail the drivers dreaded most. It was the driest, often the hottest, invariably the dustiest— or alternatively so muddy as to be barely passable. The stage often made the trip through this Bitter Creek area at night. Since the altitude in this area is between six and seven thousand feet, it can be cold at night, even in the summer, and numbingly so in the winter. And the wind is virtually incessant.

Numb from cold, or enervated by heat, bruised by the pounding lurch of the coach, fearful of suffocating in alkali dust, few passengers found much to enjoy in the scenery of the high country desert. Most passengers saw only desolate, worthless land. But it wasn't really worthless, according to an anecdote evidently popular at the time and repeated in at least one of the guidebooks that sprouted quickly after the transcontinental tour became popular. A weary and dusty tourist despondently asks, "Of what earthly use is this awful country?" "Well," drawls a station denizen, "it helps hold the two ends of the country together."

The verdict about the Bitter Creek area has been virtually unanimous; travelers found it dreadfully dreary in stagecoaches at five to ten miles an hour, and still find it so in autos at fifty-five to seventy. But this wilderness has an appeal, if one looks for it—at the right time. Samuel Bowles, editor of the Springfield, Massachusetts, *Republican*, remembered from his stage journey the rich beauty that appeared under the moonlight when the harsh outlines were softened. And there is haunting appeal in the pastel-tinted landscape of long shadows at twilight or dawn. Bowles also described the buttes that soared above the desert here and there, especially Church Butte: "the most marvelous counterfeit of a half-ruined, gigantic, old-world Gothic cathedral . . . one of the great natural wonders of the continent." The stage circled to the north of Church Butte, and Interstate Highway 80 followed much the same course a century later.

Stage drivers also disliked the Bitter Creek section of the trail for the troublesome characters they sometimes encountered there. When they had occasion to mention some man they disliked, they would frequently refer to him as a "son-of-a-bitch from Bitter Creek." Five outlaws held up one of Holladay's stages near Bitter Creek in 1865. The stage was reportedly hauling a strong box of treasure, not otherwise identified, chained to the coach under the driver's seat. Another time Holladay himself was held up during one of his trips through the Bitter Creek wasteland in one of his own stages. Ben admitted he gave up several hundred

Buttes were guiding landmarks for early travelers on the trails across Wyoming. This terraced butte is located a few miles east of Bridger's Pass. *Photo by Author.*

dollars from his pockets, but he bragged later how he kept $40,000 secreted in a money belt.

One of the stage stations showed some promise of becoming a major development—for this wilderness at least. This was the Almond Station on the south side of Bitter Creek. The partially restored rock buildings of the station are still there, directly south of the present wayside stop on Interstate 80 called Point of Rocks, which is situated on the north side of the creek. This station was a junction point for another stageline that headed off to the north for the South Pass gold mines, a heavily used line during the gold rush that brought some two thousand persons in 1867 and 1868. However, these mines were not big producers; the briefly boisterous mining camps were little more than ghosts within three years.

Almond Stage Station at Point of Rocks, east of Rock
Springs. *Photo by Author.*

The last person to reside in the Almond Station is believed to
have been Jim McKee, reportedly a onetime member of Butch
Cassidy's outlaw gang. This was long after the stageline gave way
to the railroad. People said old Jim stayed there because he was
spending his time digging for the loot stolen in a train holdup at a
place called Tipton. The treasure was supposedly buried
somewhere around Point of Rocks, but no one, including McKee,
could remember precisely where, because the cache had been
made during a drunken celebration. Jim died, poor, in 1946.

Another of the stage stations on the Overland Trail was a
crude rock structure about one mile north of the point where
Stansbury sighted his first coal seam along Bitter Creek. The stage
station was established there because someone had stumbled upon
a freshwater spring, an astonishing novelty in this country. The

water bubbled from rocks at the foot of a sandstone bluff just steps away from a now-and-then watercourse, a tributary of Bitter Creek, known as Killpecker Creek.

A favorite story in Rock Springs has it that a pony express rider discovered the spring when he was forced off his customary course by a band of Indians. The dashing and theatrical pony express lasted for only eighteen months in 1860 and 1861 before it was strangled to death, in effect, by wire, the wire of the first transcontinental telegraph line. The pony express riders followed the South Pass trail and normally never came closer than thirty-five miles of Bitter Creek. The detour to avoid the Indians would have been a major one. There seems to be no solid documentation for this pony express story. But Rock Springs clings to the story anyway, maybe because it lets some of the romance of the pony express touch the town's history. Rock Springs never fully shared in the most romantic aspects of the Frontier West.

In any case the rock spring was no longer a secret by 1862 when the stage began coming through. Today a small stone monument marks the approximate spot where the stage station and the rock spring, long since dried up, were located. The monument, often half hidden by weeds, sand, or snow, is planted along a street called Springs Drive about a quarter mile south of the point where today's Interstate Highway 80 crosses over railroad tracks and Killpecker Creek in north Rock Springs.

The swing station at the rock spring was about sixty feet long and twenty-five feet wide. It included housing for both the stock tender and the teams, the latter about as comfortably housed as the former. There were portholes in the walls about every twelve feet for rifle barrels. Stations were commonly constructed of logs, often plastered with mud, and had sod roofs. But rock was plentiful along Bitter Creek, and no farther away than the bluff at the station's rear, while logs were unavailable, unless hauled from great distances. The tamped earth formed the floor.

Because of the precious water from the spring the rock station became a small mecca of sorts for the cross-country freighters and migrant caravans. The tender for the stagecoach teams would offer to water the horses or oxen of migrants for ten cents a head.

12

Monument at the site of the Rock Spring Stage
Station. *Photo by Author.*

This traffic at the stage station attracted the attention of Archibald and Duncan Blair, brothers who had tried digging for gold in California and at the South Pass City area, where they had had some luck. But they decided to seek possibilities for profit elsewhere. Archibald thought the stage station at the rock spring might be the place. The Blair brothers took over the stage station, added a stockade, a trading post, and a wayside inn with crude bunks for the weary and venison steaks and coffee for the hungry.

Enterprising Archie Blair recognized the potential of other resources in the area as well. Like Stansbury, he noticed the conspicuous black streaks across the face of some of the bluffs overlooking Bitter Creek. He selected one of these, hired some help, and began digging. By 1868 when he was in his early thirties, he had established the first coal mine in the district at a site south of Bitter Creek, about three miles from the rock spring and the Blair stockade and trading post. Before long he also had a house there and a restaurant, the beginnings of a settlement, and he called it Blairtown.

2

The Coming of the Railroad

Before Archie Blair opened the first coal mine along Bitter Creek, talk of a railroad coming must have spread along the stageline to the station beside the rock spring. The Union Pacific Railroad Company had been created by act of Congress in 1862, after years of debate over the dream of a transcontinental line. The Union Pacific was to build, Congress said, westward from the Missouri River while the Central Pacific of California built eastward from Sacramento. In the midst of a civil war, however, an act of Congress was not enough to make it happen, even with a promise of government subsidy in land grants and loans through government bonds.

When the surrender at Appomattox in April 1865 released the nation's attention and energies, most importantly manpower, for things other than warfare, one project that awaited its attention was the proposed rail link between east and west. About three months after the historic event at Appomattox, the Union Pacific finally got its first rails spiked to ties at Omaha near the forty-first parallel of latitude. The forty-first parallel runs about forty miles south of the rock spring! In 1865 it was not yet decided precisely what route through the Rocky Mountain West the rails would take, but logic, some people argued, favored a path roughly similar to that used since 1862 by the Overland Stageline.

As late as April 1866 the westbound stagecoaches of Holladay's Overland Mail and Express Company were still leaving from Omaha. Then, the railroad's tracklaying gathered speed, and by August 20 the rails were stretched across the plains of Nebraska far enough so trains could run to Fort Kearney. Holladay moved his eastern stage terminal to Kearney, and it was obvious it would have to move farther west as the end-of-track leapfrogged west. Holladay was aware of Union Pacific plans; he was both a U.P. stockholder and one of the men named by Congress to a government board of commissioners to oversee the railroad's operations. He decided to act before his stageline was made worthless. On November 1, 1866, he sold out to Wells Fargo and Company for $1,500,000 in cash and $300,000 in Wells, Fargo stock, which he shortly also sold. Events were to prove the wisdom of his decision.

In July 1867 the railroad marked out a new town in Dakota Territory on railroad land by government grant. This would be the new division point and temporary construction headquarters. It was named Cheyenne. About six weeks later the first advertisements appeared in the Denver newspapers announcing that the railroad was ready to sell lots in the new town, but word was already out that this would be the next "end-of-track" town, so the fringe elements eager for the excitement—and money—of the place where the action would be, were scrambling into Cheyenne. Cheyenne succeeded Julesburg, which in turn had succeeded North Platte, as the "terminopolis," as some called it. On November 1, 1867, the *Leader*, Cheyenne's first newspaper, in business less than two months, reported that "Julesburg continues to arrive by ox train." The editor estimated the population of Cheyenne then, before the tracks had arrived, at four thousand persons.

As the tracks neared Cheyenne, surveying crews were far out ahead, searching for the rest of the route, planting stakes to guide graders, bridge builders, and finally the tracklayers. These advance survey crews, often small in number, were especially exposed to the dangers posed by hostile Indians and the hardships inherent in an indifferent and inhospitable land.

This was demonstrated by two groups in the year 1867. One reconnaissance party, led by Thomas Bates, had disappeared into the Great Divide Basin, a large sunken area encircled by two branches of the Continental Divide. The divide separates at a point near South Pass, one branch twisting east and then south while the other meanders south first and then back to the east. The two join again to reform a single divide at Bridger's Pass, south of Rawlins. The less than ten meager inches of precipitation a year that falls into this basin, which is about eighty miles across, drains from all sides toward the center and never escapes, except by evaporating or disappearing into the dry sandy soil. A large section of the basin, where Bates and his party had disappeared, is known as the Red Desert. A nearly level area, called a playa, at the bottom of the basin is sometimes covered with water, called Red Lake. When the water of the lake evaporates, it leaves a deposit of sediment the color of red brick.

Another survey party of about forty had gone west across the southeastern corner of the basin, staking out the line for rails that would lead to Bitter Creek, for it was clear now that this was the route the railroad would take. The leader of this party, civil engineer Percy Browne, and eight cavalrymen, were scouting ahead when they were attacked by Indians, believed to be Sioux. Forming a ring on the top of a knoll, Browne and the soldiers fought off repeated attacks, but lost all their horses, and Browne was wounded in the stomach. After the Indians withdrew, the soldiers devised a litter with carbines and blankets to carry Browne fifteen miles to the LaClede Stage Station, where he died.

A few days later a search party looking for Bates, found him and his men, sun-scorched, lost, and frantic for decent water, stumbling across the bleak basin of the Red Desert.

The tracklayers finally pushed their way into Cheyenne on November 18, 1867, and a large share of the residents of the new town abandoned their usual pursuits to line the railroad grade and watch as the town's band played rousing marches. It was a sight worth watching because by this time the tracklaying had been polished into an efficient system with characteristics of a military drill. There was good reason for that. The tracklayers had been trained by a stocky, bearded thirty-five-year-old who was only five feet four inches tall. "General Jack" the tracklayers called him. As John S. Casement he had served with the Union forces throughout the Civil War and had been brevetted a brigadier general for merit on the battlefield at Franklin, Tennessee. He and his brother Dan were experienced railroad builders and they had signed an agreement in 1866 to take over the U.P. tracklaying. While Jack bossed the track crew, Dan took charge of logistics, making certain material and personnel were available where and when needed.

Jack Casement had divided his tracklaying crew into sections of specialists and made a precise ritual out of the work assigned to each section. With much of the population of Cheyenne as audience, the tracklayers staged one of their best shows. First came brawny men who set the ties in place. They were followed by the "iron men" who lifted the new rails just laid. Two rails at a time came off the car, five men to a rail, striding forward in unison. On the command of "down" they dropped the rails into place on the ties. Next came a crew to pry the rails into line, and finally the spike drivers went to work with heavy sledges, three strokes to a spike, ten spikes to a rail, and another section of track was in place.

Cheyenne was crowded and raucous with those seeking or providing diversions. This latest end-of-track town had longer to develop than North Platte or Julesburg because Cheyenne played the role over the winter hiatus when tracklaying was halted. Since the end-of-track town moved periodically with the construction crew it had acquired the nickname of "Hell on Wheels." A story spread of a drunken man who boarded a train in Nebraska and told the conductor he wanted to go to hell. The conductor sold him a ticket to Cheyenne, where hundreds drank, gambled, and danced each night in the Headquarters Saloon, a tent 36 feet wide and 100 feet long, and where there were also seventeen variety halls each offering saloon, song-and-dance theater, and brothel under one roof.

With spring, tracklaying resumed and soon cleared the summit of the Black Hills west of Cheyenne. The rails then stretched down to the Laramie plains and across those immense grasslands to begin the climb up the eastern slope of the Continental Divide. Casement's crews were racing to outdo the Central Pacific in miles of track laid because each mile meant more government subsidy.

Much of the underworld element in Cheyenne packed up again and scrambled ahead, first to the town of Laramie, and then on to another railroad creation, the infamous "Hell on Wheels" town that lasted less than three months but, in that short life, established a reputation as the most hellish town of them all. That was Benton, named for Senator Thomas Hart Benton of Missouri, a powerful promoter of the railroad to the Pacific.

The Union Pacific platted the town of Benton next door to Fort Steele, an army post established in June 1868 on the banks of the North Platte. The garrison of three hundred at Fort Steele was to guard the railroad construction and protect the old stageline while it still ran.

When the track reached Benton in July it was about halfway across the new territory of Wyoming, created that same month by action of Congress and President Johnson. As the new rail terminus, Benton almost overnight reached a population of three thousand crowded into temporary structures of canvas or pine wood, with some fronts painted to simulate brick or brownstone. The town's water was hauled by wagon from the North Platte, three miles away, and sold for a dollar a barrel or ten cents a bucket. A shot of whiskey, reportedly the "tangle-foot" variety, cost twenty-five cents (two bits).

Only "drouth and desolation" surrounded Benton, a newspaper correspondent named John Hanson Beadle wrote. At sundown, he heard "the lively notes of the violin and guitar calling citizens to evening diversions," which meant any one of twenty-three saloons, including the "big tent," which had been moved up from Cheyenne to serve as the "great public resort of Benton." Newspaper editor Samuel Bowles also visited Benton in its brief heyday and he described it as a "congregation of scum and wickedness . . . on the alkali plain . . . by day disgusting, by night dangerous . . . averaging a murder a day."

When Benton collapsed it simply disappeared. Other end-of-track towns, North Platte, Julesburg, Cheyenne, Laramie, survived as appendages to the railroad and as service centers for other enterprises as well. But not Benton; nobody wanted to stay

UNION PACIFIC CONSTRUCTION TRAIN 1868

Union Pacific construction train and crew, 1868. For
coolness the men often slept on top of the cars.
Sweetwater County Historical Museum.

there, although a lasting settlement did sprout just a few miles
farther west at Rawlins Springs (now simply Rawlins).

There was no rest for the tracklaying crew at Benton.
Competition with the Central Pacific was now even more
aggravated. They pushed up and over the divide, about fifteen
miles north of Bridger's Pass, and labored down the gentle slope of
the Great Divide Basin into the driest section of the route, the Red
Desert, during the hottest part of the summer. It was August
when Gen. Jack Casement wrote his wife, "We haul all our water
about fifty miles on the cars." There was never enough water
under the intense sun in what Casement termed "awful country."
Lack of water may have contributed to the deaths of a number of
mules. And the men feared the rattlesnakes; crew bosses sent
youngsters ahead with six-shooters to clear out the snakes.
Despite all the problems, the rails were advanced more than sixty-
five miles during August.

Near the jutting flat-top butte known as Table Rock the
surveyors' stakes led southwest into the valley of Bitter Creek.
The pace was stepped up to three, then four, even five miles of

Looking east from the east edge of Rock Springs, Bitter Creek and its valley in 1985, with the railroad and I-80 between creek and hills. It was along this same route that the Overland Trail and the original U.P. tracks came. *Photo by Author.*

new track a day despite the scorching heat. Soon the rails were at Point of Rocks where trains could deposit freight and passengers for transfer to stages that bounced north through the Great Divide Basin to the South Pass gold diggings.

Up ahead speculators had already laid out what they called Green River City. With unbounded optimism, founders of western towns began calling a place a city as soon as they staked out lots. Here on the banks of the Green they figured the railhead would have to rest temporarily, and they were certain of the location because they found a U.P. crew preparing abutments for a bridge. When the rail layers were working their way past the site of Blairtown around October 1, 1868, it was estimated there were already two thousand persons, most of them former denizens of Benton, at the "city" on the Green, buying lots, erecting tents and shabby buildings, opening stores, setting up bars and gambling tables.

One who opted early for the Green River site was an unreconstructed southern rebel named Legh R. Freeman, who with his brother Fred had started publishing a weekly newspaper at Fort Kearney, Nebraska, in 1865, when the Union Pacific came through there. But rather than stay in Kearney, the Freemans and their *Frontier Index* moved with the "Hell on Wheels," providing a hell-raising newspaper for each succeeding town at the end of the track. The *Index* was published with a Green River dateline August 11, 1868, when the printing plant was still in Benton. Freeman wrote in that issue, "Whenever the business of this place [Green River] demands it, we will have the whole of it [that is the printing plant] come on here and then start a daily paper." In that same issue Freeman noted that Green River "is the seventh railroad town we have been at since we opened up at Kearney."

The track was coming, faster than ever. Along Bitter Creek the sweating crews laid down six miles of track between dawn and dusk one day. A few days later the Central Pacific laid seven miles on the Utah desert in a fourteen-hour performance. One October day the U.P. gang met that challenge: by starting before sunup they completed seven and one-half miles by sunset.

On October 6 the rails reached the Green, and after crossing the bridge already in place for them, the tracklayers kept right on going for thirteen miles before the Union Pacific laid out its own town and called it Bryan; that, rather than Green River City, served as the next end-of-track spot. Later, when the rails neared the Utah border, the railroad platted yet another new town, Bear River City, located west of Fort Bridger, near the present town of Evanston.

An inhabitant of Green River City, in a letter published in the *Cheyenne Leader*, October 31, 1868, reported: "The history of the rise and fall of Green River is ready to be written. Shooting and violence have characterized the short existence of the place, which has been both brief and poetic, and is played out. By Monday next there will not be 25 persons in the once famous city. The business portion of the community now consists of one house, one whiskey mill, one billiard hall and an outfitting store which is already packing up to leave." Well, the future turned out not to be quite so grim as that report seemed to portend. Green River survived and eventually became the division point for the railroad, while Bryan became only a memory.

One who had pulled out of Green River City was Legh Freeman. The daily newspaper he had promised never got started, and a headline in the weekly announced his latest plan: "Off for Bear River." The first edition of the Bear River *Frontier Index* was dated October 13, 1868. A month later the *Index* met its Appomattox.

The outspoken Freeman had never concealed his un-surrendered sympathies for the Confederate South. One of his favorite targets was the North's great Civil War hero, Ulysses S. Grant, who in 1868 was the Republican party's candidate for president.

While the nation counted votes that elected Grant, trouble brewed in Bear River City where three young men had been jailed on accusations of strangling and robbing citizens. The government for the new Wyoming Territory had not yet been organized, so where was justice to come from? The Bear River vigilantes did not wait to learn; they took the three men out of jail and lynched them. But the lynched ones had friends among the graders laboring on the railroad west of Bear River City, and they came to town bent on revenge. Their confrontation with the forces of law and order resulted in several being placed in the town's log cabin jail. This spread the indignation among the railroad construction crews.

Perhaps as many as two hundred from the U.P. construction gangs led by a huge Irishman named Magee marched into town armed with shovels and pick handles. They freed their fellow workers, burned the jail, and then, evidently figuring to settle all scores, they marched on the office of the *Frontier Index*.

Legh Freeman had editorially supported the vigilante action and infuriated many of the graders who were Union army veterans by his slanders against General Grant. He had just published a postelection edition in which he had referred to Grant as "the whiskey bloated, squaw ravishing adulterer, nigger worshipping mogul rejoicing over his election to the presidency."

But Freeman had been forewarned, so he was already headed east for Fort Bridger, by then an official U.S. Army post, going so fast, one witness asserted, one could have played checkers on his coattails. The disappointed mob vented its wrath on the printing press and other equipment in Freeman's shop, and that was the end of the *Frontier Index*.

Meanwhile, the forces of law and order had managed to organize a counterattack, and they had guns. The rioters were chased out of town and Bear River City turned to the task of assessing the damages. How many died we still do not know. Legh Freeman said forty, according to a newspaper account published in Salt Lake City, but how he would know is open to question. One who claimed to be an eyewitness said fifty-three were killed. Other estimates ranged downward to only the two who were lynched.

That fury of November in Bear River City seems to have amounted to little more than a temporary diversion for the railroad construction crews, as they plunged into the final frenzied struggle to finish as many miles of railroad as possible.

On May 10, 1869, a train could move all the way from Omaha to California, or the reverse. The tracks of the Union Pacific had been joined to those of the Central Pacific at Promontory Point, Utah. The news that the last spike had been hammered into place flashed east and west by telegraph, setting off a series of celebrations that included 100-gun salutes in New York City and Omaha and a four-mile-long parade in Chicago. The celebrating was less extravagant in the towns along the tracks in Wyoming, but it was here that the railroad was to be a dominating economic and political force. A special census taken in Wyoming in 1869 revealed that more than 85 percent of the eight thousand white persons counted in the territory lived in communities along the U.P. railroad.

The completed railroad was, in effect, the long-sought Northwest Passage—a speedy way across the continental barrier. Trains leaving from Omaha and Sacramento took five days between the two cities; travel by wagon had taken about two months; trips on the horse-drawn stages about three weeks. The impact of the railroad was felt immediately in various ways. Wells, Fargo had to sell off about $50,000 worth of stagecoaches, horses, and gear at about one-third of cost. West Coast merchants found their shelves burdened by over-priced products, reflecting wagon freight rates across the continent: about $1.80 per hundred pounds per hundred miles. The railroads in 1869 were charging $7.50 per hundred pounds first class freight all the way from Chicago to California. Collapse of a number of freight wagon companies threw hundreds of men out of work.

On the other hand there were gains. The railroad made the job of frontier defense by the army easier, more efficient, and cheaper. The railroad fostered new businesses, including eventually the open-range livestock industry in Wyoming. It also promptly propagated coal mining with its inevitable grimy and company-controlled towns. And, since the first transcontinental passenger service was inaugurated only five days after the final spikes were driven in Utah, the railroad brought an almost immediate surge of tourists, who like earlier travelers by covered wagon and stagecoach found Wyoming mostly a desolation to be crossed, not a destination.

The Railway Act of 1864 granted the railroad possession of any coal found in its land grants, and coal in fact was known to exist along the planned route. In 1868 some of the directors of the U.P. company negotiated a contract with a man named Thomas Wardell and his associate, C.O. Godfrey, to prospect for, open, and operate coal mines on railroad land-grant sections along the tracks. The contract provided that the railroad would pay, in the first year, $6.00 a ton for the coal Wardell and Godfrey produced. The price would drop from there at prescribed steps to $3.00 a ton for the last six years of the fifteen-year contract. It was estimated that the cost of mining the coal would be about $2.00 a ton in the beginning and would eventually decrease to nearly one-half that amount.

A corporation called the Wyoming Coal and Mining Company surfaced in January 1869, under Nebraska law, and this company, it developed, had the U.P. coal contract, assigned to it by Wardell, who had bought out partner Godfrey. Wardell held one-tenth of the $500,000 capital stock in this company of which he was superintendent, secretary, and general manager. All the rest of the stock belonged to six directors of the Union Pacific Railroad Company. Therefore, a major portion of the profits, which were certain to be considerable under the terms of the contract, would be diverted to these few U.P. directors.

The contract allowed Wardell to sell coal commercially to buyers other than the Union Pacific, and the railroad would rebate to him 25 percent of freight charges for any such coal hauled by the Union Pacific. Wardell was to pay the railroad a royalty because it owned the coal.

When the railroad route was being surveyed, Gen. Grenville Dodge, chief engineer for construction of the Union Pacific, said the Bitter Creek country "has no inviting qualities" except "all of it is underlaid with immense beds of coal." Immense was not an exaggeration. It is estimated today that beneath 96 percent of Sweetwater County, Wyoming, there are layers of coal sandwiched between layers of sandstone, limestone, and clay. Some of these coal seams, however, lie at great depths, as much as three thousand feet below the surface. These deepest layers have never been reached by even the most sophisticated of modern coal mining techniques.

At least 100 million years ago, the region we now call southwestern Wyoming was covered by a huge sea that swelled and shrank many times in a climate that was warm and humid, fostering swamplike and very dense tropical forests of huge plants—giant ferns, trees up to one hundred feet tall, and perhaps a tangle of undergrowth. As the level of the water rose and fell repeatedly in cycles that required hundreds of years, the vegetation repeated a cycle too, dying and sinking into the muck of the sea bottom to form thick layers of organic material. During long periods of high-water levels, sand and silt washed off the surrounding dry land and after settling over the layers of plants eventually solidified into sandstone or limestone. This process was repeated a number of times creating many layers of plant material between layers of stone. The great weight of the stone compacted the plant material, squeezing most of the water out, until peat was formed, and then with the pressure of more layers of stone and more centuries of time, the peat became coal. Twenty feet of original plant material formed about one foot of coal.

The vast extent of the coal deposits was indicated in the first thorough geological survey of the area by the U.S. government. This survey identified at least thirty-seven distinct coal beds, but about one-half of those were too thin to be of commercial value. This same general process of plants as well as dead animals—fish, repitiles, and dinosaurs—settling into layers between sedimentary rocks also brought about petroleum and natural gas.

Following this long period in which various layers of materials were deposited, came a period of upheaval that geologists call the Laramide Revolution when explosive volcanic eruptions hurled lava flows over the land and sulfurous clouds of ash through the air. At the same time tremendous pressures tried to compress the earth's crust, and the crust buckled upward. This upheaval of the land forty million years ago, or thereabouts, created the land formations we call the Rocky Mountains, including the dome or uplift in the area where Rock Springs is situated today. The Rock Springs dome extends for about ninety miles north and south and for about fifty miles east and west. The Leucite Hills mark the northern end of the dome and Aspen Mountain the southern end.

Wyoming never shared to any significant degree in the bonanzas of gold and silver mining in the American West, but the state was provided with a geological storehouse of riches of another sort. This vast wasteland that for more than a century seemed to travelers so uselessly and drably barren, and may still seem so to motorists today, has contributed and has much left to contribute in precious natural resources, including the vast coal deposits in the Rock Springs dome. Water and wind have eroded away much of the dome, slicing down through the various layers of the earth's crust, creating the large Baxter Basin through the dome's center, and exposing to the view of Stansbury and others the precious seams of coal.

Shacks and outhouses along Bitter Creek in north Rock Springs. Note the way the dugout at left is built into the bank with water barrel on top of bank. *Western History Research Center, University of Wyoming.*

3

In the Beginning

About three months before the Wyoming Coal and Mining Company was created and at least six months before the linkup at Promontory Point completed the transcontinental rail route, Union Pacific locomotives were burning their first Wyoming coal. Thomas Wardell had set his miners digging in the summer of 1868 on a sagebrush hillside south of the newly installed U.P. tracks and east of the Continental Divide. Their shaft hit a rich coal seam eighty-five feet below the surface, and they soon had a hoist installed and a camp established; they called it Carbon. The Carbon mine produced 6,560 tons of coal during the rest of that year and produced more than four and one-half million tons before it was closed in 1902. Only a few cemetery markers are left at the Carbon site today, about fourteen miles west of the present town of Medicine Bow.

But one producing mine was not enough to satisfy either the U.P. directors or Wardell, so while he supervised work at Carbon Thomas, sent his brother, Charles, to prospect farther west, accompanied by a veteran expert in coal mining from Lancashire, England, William H. Mellor. They found a number of outcrops along Bitter Creek and at least three mines were opened, one at a spot called Hallville, another near a pair of prominent landmarks known as Black Buttes, and the third at Point of Rocks.

Charlie Wardell and Bill Mellor realized that these were only test mines; they might not prove out, so they moved on west a few miles to poke about in the area where Stansbury had reported a number of outcrops eighteen years earlier. The spot on a slope above the south bank of Bitter Creek where they agreed to make another try was not one Stansbury had noticed, but Mellor thought it promising. The stage station and its freshwater spring were about two miles north of their chosen spot, but they named their new coal camp Rock Spring anyway. (The final *s* was added some time later.) They brought in a crew of miners, and before the end of 1868 this mine, later to be called No. 1, had produced 365 tons of coal. In the next year, its first full year of operation, the mine produced almost 17,000 tons. Two years later this site outproduced the mine at Carbon with more than 40,000 tons.

Without benefit of the sophisticated coal-prospecting techniques and tools developed later, Mellor and Charlie Wardell had discovered one of the finest seams in the fabulously coal-rich area geologically described as the Rock Springs dome or uplift. The layer or seam of coal they tapped was ten to twelve feet thick between a layer of shale above and sandstone below. The seam ran in a northwesterly direction, sloping gently downward with a twelve-foot drop in every one hundred feet. Their guesses at where to dig and in what direction were perfect. Nor could they have found a mine more convenient to its intended customer. The U.P.'s mainline track, laid through the Rock Spring area as the mine was being opened, was placed along the south bank of Bitter Creek and just a few yards north of the mine entry. The rails and much of the coal camp and the town it subsequently became were built directly over the tunnels of this mine that eventually reached more than one-half million tons in annual production. For forty-one years this mine was a major producer from a main slope that eventually penetrated the earth for one and one-half miles from the entrance. The lower entries or levels extended for another one and one-half miles on either side of the main slope.

The mine company and railroad officials soon knew that the coal from this Rock Spring No. 1 mine, jet black, with a glassy luster and occasional iridescent colors, was a high-quality bituminous, nearly ideal for the railroad's locomotives. The coal burned well under forced draft, but it did produce lots of sparks, and this caused some troublesome fires along the tracks until the railroad developed special grates to control the sparking. The coal did not produce clinkers and left relatively little ash. Wardell ordered the mining company's efforts concentrated at Rock

Spring No. 1 and at Carbon. The mines at Hallville, Black Buttes, and Point of Rocks were abandoned.

Prominent in the early mining crew at Rock Spring were hardy, experienced miners from the British Isles, primarily from northern England and Scotland, and a few from Wales. Like Mellor, the Lankie (from Lancashire), the Wardell brothers were from northern England. British miners began arriving in the coal fields of eastern and midwestern United States about 1850. Later some moved on west to Wyoming Territory where, in 1870, immigrants from the British Isles accounted for about one-fifth of the total population, and more than one-half of the foreign-born.

Two Scotsmen who helped open the No. 1 mine were George L. Young, Sr. and Ross Dickson. Both were popular among the exclusively male population of the early coal camp and among the expanded mixed population later. Dickson spent the rest of his life in Rock Springs, except for brief visits back to Scotland.

Young was often referred to as "Geordie" and sometimes as "Wee Geordie," because he was a small man. (But maybe no one called him that to his face.) Geordie opened a second mine in the camp known as Rock Spring at a point less than a mile southwest of No. 1 but soon sold it to Wardell's U.P.-supported company; it then became known as the U.P. No. 2 mine at Rock Springs. (The final *s* had been added by this time.) Geordie, with a partner named John Jarvie, next opened one of the first general merchandise stores in the expanding camp while he also worked as a coal prospector for a number of companies. He then tried the Klondike goldfields for two unsuccessful years before returning to Rock Springs where he died in 1915.

American coal companies, for the most part, adopted the British mining system, which was a form of industrial feudalism transported, like most of the workers, from the old world to the new. Under this system, miners were paid so much per bushel or per ton of coal produced. They had to buy their own tools—pick, shovel, and drill—and explosive powder to blast the coal free. These work necessities, as well as clothing and food, were usually purchased on credit from a store either owned or authorized by the company.

Underground there was a minimum of supervision; the miners worked in pairs in whatever fashion they pleased and as steadily as they pleased. The more experienced hand usually swung the pick, did the drilling, and set the charges. His buddy, often an apprentice and not infrequently a youngster starting out as young as nine or ten, wielded the shovel. When the miners got their families to Rock Springs, many took their sons into the mines as trainee partners, just as they would have done in England. Geordie and his son, Jack, formed one such pair. Geordie never carried a watch; he never had need for one, he said, because "Jack knows when quitting time comes better than any watch that was ever made."

It was not only arduous work, but hazardous, although in Rock Springs somewhat less so than in the mines of the British Isles and the midwestern United States. Explosive gases were seldom encountered at dangerous levels in the Rock Springs mines; there was never an explosion in the No. 1 mine during its forty-one years of operation. But injuries and deaths from rock falls and other forms of accidents were common.

The mines fostered pride, individualism, and a cohesive sense of oneness. Coal miners thought of themselves, quite accurately, as a unique group. This helps explain their extraordinary support of unionism in later years. In Rock Springs these burly, usually bearded men lived in an isolated community, struggled against rock and coal under prolonged discomfort for about one-half of every twenty-four hours, and then emerged from the pits only to plod into miserable shacks that were themselves partly buried in the land and lighted only by coal oil lamps or candles. The miners built their hovels with the rear wall tight against the bank of Bitter Creek; the building rested on a bar of mud and sand, at the most a foot or two above the level of the water. Usually the roof was only another few inches above the top of the creek bank. As a result these "dugouts," as they were called, seemed part of the landscape.

Each new workday the miners donned the same blackened, dusty clothes they had worn out of the mine the day before. There was no communal bathhouse. Usually they bathed once a week in a galvanized tub by the dugout's heating and cooking stove. The working day for Dickson, Young, and the other miners at the first Rock Spring mine started before sunup and, in the winter at least, ended after sundown. Twelve hours or more were the norm, and they worked a full week; seven days were not unusual.

Before they left for work it was necessary to light the lamps they wore on their caps to illuminate their way in the predawn darkness. It was an oil lamp with a cotton wick, and in a pocket they carried a short, thin pick of iron to lift up the wick when it burned down. As the miners trudged off to work these lamps, which gave little illumination and much ill-smelling smoke, formed meandering lines of flickering lights along the often snow-covered paths that took whatever routes might be convenient and reasonably direct to the mouth of No. 1. Some of these paths later developed into streets.

The miners descended into the inky blackness of the long entry slope to the rooms they had been assigned and usually began work by shoveling into a pit car the chunks of coal that had been blasted loose by the powder exploded at the end of the previous day. Loaded cars were lowered down a slight slope to the main entry where a driver hitched them behind his mule to pull them out of the mine to the tipple. There all cars were recorded by numbered metal tags placed on them by the miners, thus identifying who should get payment for the labor. The early miners were paid seven cents for each bushel of coal. Later, after the company installed scales, pay was based on tonnage. The first miners at No. 1 made about $2.00 a day, high wages for the 1870s. There was a standard deduction for slack, because the railroad could not use slack coal then nor could the company sell it to any other coal users.

Underground each pair of miners worked independently in separate rooms carved out of the coal seam. Before they could blast any coal loose they had to first cut a gash or "kerf" about five feet deep under one wall (called a "face") of the room. To do this a miner lay on his side in the thick carpet of coal dust covering the sandstone floor from which the seam of coal had already been removed. He swung his pick at floor level to cut the gash. As he pulled out the coal his pick knocked loose, he was nearly buried in

Two views of coal mining from two eras. Top shows miner swinging a pick as he lies on floor of mine room to dig out the kerf. Young man at left drills hole for blasting powder. These were methods of the early period of mining in Rock Springs. Bottom photo shows an early electrical cutting machine doing the job of undercutting the wall of coal in a later period. *Sweetwater County Historical Museum.*

slack. Then he cut a vertical gash either at one corner or through the center of the face.

Next he drilled holes above the kerf with a breast auger, a drill several feet long with a broad plate at the end opposite the bit. The miner pressed his breast against this plate as he turned the bit. Once the necessary number of holes were drilled, black powder was tamped into each with a long needle; "dummies" or packing sealed up the opening except for the small hole left by the needle when it was withdrawn. Through this hole the "squib" or fuse was inserted, then lighted. The miners would then scurry out of the room until after the blast.

Digging out the kerf and then blasting the coal loose was known as mining "in the clear." "Shooting off the solid" (without the kerf) was prohibited. Miners were sometimes fired for this because it resulted in finely shattered coal and a great deal of useless slack. The slack coal as well as any rock, slate, or dirt was supposed to be separated from the chunk coal and discarded in a corner of the room; that was the "gob pile." During lunch period the miners would gather on one of the gob piles with their lunch buckets for jokes, gossip, and discussion of any matter of general concern. More than one union leader started his career on a gob pile.

The census of 1870 counted just 117 persons in Rock Springs; in 1880 the count was 763. Two factors accounted for this increase: two new mines were opened, providing jobs for more miners, and most of the residents of Blairtown moved over to Rock Springs.

The Blairs had tried to continue selling their coal but their only customers were a few who were not employed by the Union Pacific and could be reached by wagon. The Union Pacific did not run a spur line to the Blair mine and did not ship any Blair coal over the railroad. The Blairs finally closed their mine and concentrated on ranching.

Most of the hardy souls living in Rock Springs huddled in the dugouts where the creek bank sheltered them from the cold in the winter, the heat in the summer, and the wind year-round. It was treacherous country at times, or, as someone said, "Hell on women and horses!" Storms sometimes washed out the railroad tracks around Rock Springs or clogged them with snow between Cheyenne and Medicine Bow. The winter of 1871-72 was particularly perilous. Blizzards stalled trains during the last week of January and intermittent storms continued to slow or stop trains until April.

The coal camp grew without plan or pattern, except by that dictated by the railroad tracks, the wandering course of Bitter Creek, and the whims of the first inhabitants. It developed in this random fashion for ten years before the first efforts were made to survey a plan for streets and building lots. Business houses and frame one-story homes formed ragged lines on both sides of the railroad, the beginnings of what became North Front and South Front streets. South Front was later officially renamed South Main Street, but it is still popularly referred to as South Front. Behind the North Front Street buildings the dugouts of the miners spread haphazardly along Bitter Creek.

As mine officials established homes, beginning with one for the first mine superintendent, Bill Mellor, they were placed on the south side, along with the depot, which was a boxcar moved over from Blairtown. The south side was also the location by 1873 of the most impressive building in camp, a two-story stone structure that housed the mine office, the "company store," and the post office, which had also been moved from Blairtown.

The store, operated by the Beckwith-Quinn Company under contract with the Union Pacific Railroad, served a variety of purposes for the first few years. Since it was the only place in town that had coffins, it served as an undertaking parlor, and the store's delivery wagon served as a hearse. The store was also used for parties and community gatherings, with a counter serving for a stage when needed and the space between counters as a dance floor.

To this place they called "the big store" the miners also came with their "passbooks" in which were recorded charged purchases of groceries, clothes, mining tools, and blasting powder. Then at the first of the month, when gold and silver coins arrived by train to be doled out by the store manager acting as payroll agent for the mining company, they came again with the passbooks to see how the record of bushels of coal mined compared with their store charge accounts. Deductions were made: first, for slack; second, for what was owed the company for rent (the company owned the land and most of the houses) and for heating coal; and, finally, for any charges owed the store. The worker received what was left. Often there was very little with the result that payday was frequently a disappointment to the miners' families. But their first experience with payday would not have been their first disappointment; that must have come when they first arrived in the territory.

Some women recalled riding the train across Wyoming to join their husbands, and as they stared in dismay at the treeless landscape, an endless immensity of space sliding by the train windows, they considered the possibility of turning back. Mrs. Herbert Crofts from Leicester, England, recalled there were just three houses when she arrived in Rock Springs. "They all belonged to the mine bosses. The miners lived in dugouts along the bank of Bitter Creek." Another woman recalled wondering why so many chimney pipes seemed to be coming out of the ground. And why wasn't there at least one tree, or even a blade of grass? The children of another Rock Springs pioneer recall their mother telling them that she had wept for days for the bonnie green lands of Scotland. Like Mrs. Crofts, who moved into one of the dugouts with husband and four children, almost all the women stayed, however, and in an amazing testimony to their fortitude, not only coped but raised families in those two- or three-room dugouts. In many cases they took in boarders—bachelor miners—as well!

Rock Springs homemakers managed without piped-in water for twenty years. The murky water of Bitter Creek was unusable and the sulfurous water from the only well in town was used, as a rule, only to fill a watering trough for horses. Men such as Ed Clegg drove water wagons either to and from the spring north of town or Point of Rocks, about twenty-five miles east, until the railroad began running a water train of tank cars to Green River and back. The water was stored in barrels at each house at a cost of twenty-five cents a barrel. Dennis P. Murphy, who emigrated from Ireland in 1871, was engineer of the water train. Each day about halfway back on the return trip he stopped to eat his lunch at a place that became known as Murphy's Glen. In the winter the water sometimes froze in the tank cars and more often in the barrels, or the cows that roamed the streets drank from the barrels. Almost all the houses also had a rain barrel to collect extra water precious for washing hair, cooking, or doing laundry.

At least in Wyoming Territory women's rights were getting an unusual degree of attention, although it is not clear how much awareness there was of this in Rock Springs. The first territorial legislature in 1869 passed acts protecting the rights of women to property, to "enjoyment of the fruits of their labor," to equal pay as teachers, and, the most famous of all, an act giving women the right to vote.

The census report did not indicate the sex of the 117 inhabitants counted at Rock Springs and Blairtown in 1870; presumably they were all male. However, the men evidently were already sending for wives and children or waiting sweethearts. Archie Blair made a trip back to Canada and returned in 1870 with a bride, the first woman in Blairtown, some people insisted; but, since the first schools in the area were attempted around 1870, it seems safe to assume that there were other women with families in the area by that time or soon thereafter. An early attempt at a school—maybe the first—apparently had very few pupils since it was held in a tiny kitchen in Blairtown with Mrs. Mary A. Patterson as teacher. She used brown paper sacks pasted on boards as substitutes for blackboards. The first school in what was then the Rock Spring coal camp appears to have been held in a second-floor room above a saloon and store owned by John Jarvie and George L. Young on the north side of the tracks. A Mrs. Osborn was the teacher, succeeded by a Miss or Mrs. Holliday.

In 1874 the first schoolhouse was constructed on what is now B Street on the south side of the tracks; thirty pupils met in the single room of the frame structure. In the same year the Rock Springs school district (No. 4) was organized. Some sources indicate the first teacher in the schoolhouse was a man; if so, his tenure was brief. His successor was Mrs. James Tisdale, who taught there for eleven years. Eventually two rooms were added to the building and a second teacher, Mrs. Mary A. Clark, was hired. Mrs. Clark later was to serve as county superintendent of schools and then as city librarian.

Frequently now it was the school that was used for social and community affairs, including Christmas celebrations. One resident recalled a childhood memory of two decorated pine trees flanking the platform at one end of the largest schoolroom on Christmas Eve. The trees were acquired from the Evanston area with funds donated by the coal miners. The Union Pacific provided gifts for all the children in camp, a practice the company continued for many years; usually each child received a silver dollar and an orange or an apple.

For another celebration in 1878 Barney McCabe, the town constable, supplied the tree. Barney had come from Ireland, settled temporarily at South Pass, drove a freight wagon for a spell between South Pass and the U.P. station at Bryan, which was west of Green River, and, finally, settled in Rock Springs. He cut and hauled the 1878 Christmas tree from a mountain several miles south of town. After it was erected in one corner of the schoolroom it was decorated with candles and strings of cranberries and popcorn. One person who was there remembered at least one small string of tinsel. That evening the children, some dressed like fairies (or maybe they were intended to represent angels), provided entertainment with carols and pageantry before Santa Claus arrived. John Ludvigsen, later to be the first police court justice and the second mayor of Rock Springs, played the accordion for dancing.

An interdenominational Sunday school began meeting at the schoolhouse in 1876, organized by Solomon Rouff, Mrs. James Tisdale, and Mrs. Alice Kierle. Other early religious services were held in homes, including those of Mormons who organized the first congregation of the Church of Jesus Christ of Latter Day Saints in 1882.

The Union Congregational Church was established in 1881 and its building completed in the following year. This church struggled, with limited success, to keep its pastorate filled. Various members of the congregation, including a coal miner named Timothy Thirloway, filled the pulpit while a sparse congregation squirmed uncomfortably on hard plank pews fashioned by local woodworkers. The benches were padded with carpeting in 1890, about the time the church became the First Congregational. It was no longer a "union" of faiths because many of the original members had departed as other denominations were established.

Enough donations were collected to construct a Roman Catholic church on No. 2 Hill in 1884, but it was without a pastor until January 1888 when Father John Delahunty arrived; he ministered to a grateful and loyal flock in Rock Springs for more than sixteen years.

A number of officers and enlisted men of the U.S. Army units moved into Rock Springs in the 1880s were Episcopalians, and their arrival prompted the formation of a congregation of that faith, which met in a small hall above one of the town's most popular saloons, the Fountain Club on South Front. A member of the congregation recalled that the rector, the Reverend I.L. Morton, was fond of saying that his flock met with "spirit above and spirits below." By the time this group had its first church building in 1889 it was known as the Church of the Holy Communion.

The First Finnish Evangelical Lutheran Church survived for its first years with a part-time pastor, a Mr. H. Tanner, who rode a train from the Carbon coal camp, 140 miles to the east, to preach in Rock Springs the second Sunday of every month until he moved to the Bitter Creek camp. In January 1895 this congregation was shattered by emotional dissension over both ethical and procedural questions. The congregation of approximately two hundred was cut in half after all the "disobedient" members had been "expelled" and others, saddened by the quarreling, simply stopped attending the church services or switched to a new congregation called the National Church that met in the No. 4 district. A year later a new pastor, the Reverend Mr. Adolph Riippa of Minnesota, led a rejuvenation of the Finnish Evangelical Lutherans, but the schism in the Finnish community within Rock Springs was so deep rancor was still present nearly a century later.

The Methodists of Rock Springs held meetings in homes until they rented a lodge hall for Sunday mornings. In 1895 they bought a store building and converted it into a church.

In the first decade of Rock Springs' history finding medical attention was much more difficult than finding spiritual guidance. The nearest doctor was in Rawlins, more than 100 miles east, so most of the help for the sick or injured was supplied by the kindly and hard-working mine superintendent, William Mellor, who knew more about first aid and home remedies than most in camp. In 1880 an experienced physician from Lander, Wyoming, 120 miles northeast of Rock Springs, came through town on his way to Green River City, where he had been summoned as a witness in a murder trial. He also stopped in Rock Springs to attend a Republican party meeting, and while he was there Dr. Edward Day Woodruff patched up an injured coal miner whose friends and coworkers were sufficiently impressed to send a committee to persuade the doctor to make Rock Springs his home. Woodruff protested that he had come west to recover his health, damaged by overwork at his practice in Chicago, where he planned to return.

He finally agreed to stay for six months but he had hardly set up an office before he was advised that to stay could endanger his own health—a threat from a delegation of miners he believed had been sent by the doctor in Rawlins. Woodruff's response was to buy a gun to carry in his black medical bag as he moved about town seeing his patients. After the first six months he forgot about Chicago and stayed for ten years, during which time he became resident physician for the Union Pacific Railroad and served for two years as county superintendent of schools.

Woodruff's skills were occasionally needed to patch up a cowboy from one of the ranches scattered widely over the semidesert lands surrounding Rock Springs. A number of ranchers had town homes in Rock Springs, and some became involved in town merchandising enterprises; most were stockholders in the early banks, some serving as bank officers. Included were the Blairs; Abner Luman, a Virginian who came west as a freighter before the railroad was built; Adam Cooper, who was one of the first to get a ranch established in the area;

Joseph Henry Brooks, who arrived in the early eighties and became one of the leading bankers; Robert Taylor and Griff Edwards, among the first to stock their ranches with sheep rather than cattle; William R. Bates, who came to Wyoming at age fourteen from Texas to work as a ranch hand and stayed to be a leading rancher; Joseph Young, an Englishman who opened a butcher shop in Rock Springs and later became a rancher, county commissioner, and county sheriff; Samuel Mathews, also born in England, who owned hotels in Rock Springs and Green River before becoming a rancher and bank stockholder; the Irishman, Tim Kinney, ex-railroad agent who started a cattle ranch, became president of a bank, county commissioner, and state representative and started a general merchandise store at which, it was said, one could find anything from a needle to an anchor; and the German, William Gottsche, who arrived at the age of twenty-one to begin a career as merchant, rancher, and banker.

As the coal mining got established along Bitter Creek, the booming industrial growth that had followed the Civil War was collapsing in the eastern states. The national economy plunged into panic in September 1873, with the sudden collapse of the investment house of Jay Cooke and Company and other financial institutions. Rock Springs had suffered a setback earlier, in 1871, when the miners there and in Carbon had struck for higher pay. Thomas Wardell, president of the coal company had a simple policy for dealing with strikers—he fired them. To defeat the strike he also had the help of the federal government because he persuaded the federal officials that a show of force was needed at both Rock Springs and Carbon to protect railroad property, which, he said, was vital to the nation as a communication link. Troops from Fort Steele set up temporary tent camps in both Carbon and Rock Springs while Wardell imported new miners, this time Scandinavians, who were willing to work for the prevailing wage.

The mines were back in full production shortly and more than one hundred were at work at mines No. 1 and 2 when the coal company opened No. 3 in 1873, about one-half mile north of No. 1. This increased scale of activity in the mines largely insulated the coal camp from the impact of the depression. By the middle of the decade Rock Springs was the major coal production site for the U.P. system, producing 58,476 tons in 1874 and then nearly doubling that with 104,667 tons in 1875, despite the interruption of another strike.

By this time the Union Pacific's board of directors had recognized the importance of coal as a major source of revenue for the railroad. The estimated cost of producing coal at the U.P. mines was about $2.00 a ton. Profits that the Union Pacific could realize from selling coal that it did not burn in its own locomotives were indicated by the fact that Wardell's company sold coal in Ogden, Utah, at $6.50 a ton. At the same time other coal producers were charged by the U.P. railroad $10.00 a ton to ship their coal to Ogden. Similar figures could be quoted for Cheyenne and Omaha. Coal represented about one-fourth of all the freight carried by the road in 1874 and 1875. Abruptly the railroad officials informed Wardell that they were taking over all coal lands and mining properties, simply abrogating the contract they had made with Wardell in 1868. Wardell went to court trying to compel the railroad to honor his contract, but after five years of litigation the U.S. Supreme Court ruled the contract fraudulent from the beginning and therefore void.

The "massacre" of the Chinese at Rock Springs as
drawn by T. de Thulstrip for *Harper's Weekly* from
photographs taken by Lt. C.A. Booth, Seventh U.S.
Infantry. Published September 26, 1885. *Photo copy
made of the drawing by the Author.*

4

The Chinese Massacre

When the U.P. railroad assumed control of the coal mines it organized its own coal department, placing D.O. Clark, Wardell's former bookkeeper, in charge as general superintendent with offices in Omaha. Clark held that job for sixteen years and then continued as a top executive with the U.P. Coal Company when, as a subsidiary of the railroad, it replaced the coal department. Clark's tall, slender, and always impeccably dressed figure became familiar in Rock Springs and the other U.P. coal camps, because he visited them often on inspection tours. When he wrote out instructions the handwriting was as impeccable as his dress.

The change to control by the railroad brought no significant change in labor policy at the coal mines. That policy remained basically what was traditional in U.S. industry generally in the late nineteenth century. But circumstances in Rock Springs made confrontation between labor and management highly probably midway through the decade of the seventies.

Coal from the U.P. mines that the railroad's locomotives did not burn could be sold at a handsome profit, partly because the railroad controlled the price by charging competing coal producers high freight rates. However, the excess from the U.P. mines was small because, the company asserted, the miners worked only enough to earn the wages necessary to cover their own living expenses. The miners worked an average of only three days a week, the company said.

About a year after Clark became superintendent, the company, in an effort to force the miners to work more hours, cut the per bushel pay rate from five cents to four. At five cents a bushel the miners were earning about $1.00 a ton. Even with a 20 percent pay cut, the company contended, the approximately five hundred miners then employed in all the U.P. mines in Wyoming could earn substantially more than the average American laborer, which was true. But that did not take into account factors that were of great concern to the workers: the ten- to twelve-hour days involved and the fact that miners had to buy supplies and tools essential to their work.

The Knights of Labor, organized in Philadelphia in 1869, had finally extended its membership into Wyoming coalfields, and this link with a national labor organization of growing power plus a conviction that there was a shortage of labor encouraged militancy among the miners. Even more important was the miners' conviction that the company had reneged on a promise to offset the pay cut by reducing prices charged at the company store for tools, powder, and clothing.

As the chill of the nights deepened with the autumn of 1875, the stockpile of coal for the winter market failed to grow, but the anxiety of the company officials did. Finally, the U.P. boss in Rock Springs confronted representatives of the miners with a request that they increase production 25 percent at the four-cent per bushel rate. A meeting of the miners at the Knights of Labor hall apparently followed before their delegation returned to tell the boss that the answer was no. According to a story of an eyewitness reporter for a Cheyenne newspaper, the boss replied he would soon have "a body of men here who will dig for us all the coal we want."

Many of the miners, including those Britons who had survived the 1871 strike and some of the newer Scandinavian immigrants as well, stopped work altogether in November 1875. A "Discharge Record Book" kept by clerks of the U.P. coal department shows that ninety-nine miners in Rock Springs were fired for striking "for one cent per bushel."

Within a few days, replacement laborers were stepping off passenger trains from the west while U.P. freight trains were unloading materials for constructing houses for the new workers. Shortly mining resumed with a core of at least fifty Rock Springs veterans who had not joined the strike and at least three times that many new employees—Chinese.

The arrival of the Chinese, recruited for the coal company by the company store operators, Beckwith-Quinn, should not have been a surprise to the miners since they had been plainly told the company was prepared to replace them. In addition, it was well-known that the Union Pacific was hiring Chinese for its section crews, which did routine track maintenance. It has also hired Chinese to work in its mines at Almy in the southwestern corner of Wyoming.

About the time the first Chinese miners arrived, another group suddenly appeared because of an incident that had occurred a few days earlier. A mine boss reported a rifle bullet whizzed by his head as he was standing on the platform of the railroad depot. The shot came, he thought, from the direction of the miners' homes. This prompted an appeal from the railroad officials for help in "maintaining order and protecting lives and property." The precedent for this had been established in 1871. Governor John M. Thayer, distracted from an increasingly troublesome Indian problem in the northwestern section of the territory, took a train from Cheyenne to Rock Springs to try mediation but found both sides inflexible. Lacking territorial militia, he sent an appeal for federal troops to Gen. George Crook, recently promoted to commander of the U.S. Army's Department of the Platte. Crook, too, was preoccupied with signs of new Indian troubles, but the fierce and tragic campaigns of 1876 were still six months away. He could spare two companies from Fort Steele, and they arrived in Rock Springs by a night train; residents awoke to find carefully aligned rows of army tents spread once more in open spaces along Bitter Creek.

With the soldiers standing guard, the Chinese settled into huts hastily erected north of Bitter Creek on a sagebrush flat near the No. 3 mine and about a quarter of a mile north of the center of town. This was quickly dubbed "Chinatown," an accretion of shacks the company had put up plus additions fashioned by the occupants from old boards, packing boxes, and flattened tin cans, a new dimension to the local town's shabby ugliness.

The Union Pacific had its mines back to full production early in 1876, and then the strikers offered to return to work at the four-cent rate. The company's counter offer consisted of railroad passes for free rides to Omaha. As the unemployed left town, the soldiers struck their tents and boarded a train to return to Fort Steele.

The Chinese came from a large and willing labor pool that had started growing on the West Coast around 1850 when economic and political turbulence had magnified the misery of peasants in south China around Canton. Emigration from China was forbidden, but many men slipped out of the country to seek fortunes elsewhere to support starving families. News of the gold strikes in California started a near tidal wave of Chinese across the Pacific Ocean to what they called the Golden Mountain. By 1851 there were 25,000 in California; by 1870 there were 63,000 in the United States, most of them on the West Coast.

Few struck it rich in the goldfields, but when the Central Pacific Railroad began laying track east from California it desperately needed men for construction crews. The willing and docile Chinese provided the answer; they laid most of the Central Pacific's track to Promontory Point, Utah. When that job was completed in 1869, the Chinese needed other opportunities. One came in the coal mines of the Rocky Mountain West.

As long as the Chinese took jobs no white man wanted they were tolerated, but when they began competing for jobs the European-born workers sought, an anti-Chinese movement quickly gathered momentum. States passed laws, cities adopted ordinances, courts proclaimed special rules to curb the ability of the Chinese to compete.

There was no difficulty in establishing a rationale for this. Many of the Chinese came on the "credit-ticket" system; they pledged their labor in the United States to pay for their Pacific passage. "Slave labor," the Chinese opponents cried. (Many Europeans earned their way to America under a similar system as indentured servants.) And the Chinese were sojourners—in America only to accumulate enough money to rank as rich when they returned to China. (Of course, many Europeans had come with a similar goal in mind.) Even if the Chinese should decide they might like to stay in America, with their curious mannerisms, outlandish garb, and peculiar speech, they could never be absorbed in the great "melting pot." They clung to the customs and the culture of the country from which they came. The Chinese were in the United States, but not part of it. (Europeans, too, in the tenement districts of the cities and in some semi-isolated hamlets of the Midwest, recreated a version of their homeland life styles.)

Were the Chinese so much different from the Germans, Finns, Italians, and other Europeans also arriving in the United States in significant numbers? A Californian, writing in the *Overland Monthly*, a nationally circulated magazine, thought he saw significant differences. The Europeans, he wrote, bring families, and "sink into the body politic, and their children are not distinguishable from other native born." The Europeans, he added, "do not come or threaten to come in countless hosts, like the swarms of Attila; as a rule they bring no strange diseases, and have no unnatural vices." These arguments and scarcely veiled insinuations helped provide the climate of opinion that made it possible for states on the West Coast to pass such laws as one providing that "no Chinese shall be permitted to give evidence in favor of, or against, any white man." No wonder American vernacular adopted the phrase "a Chinaman's chance."

Before they arrived in Rock Springs the Chinese had learned ways to deal with this hostility. Among them was "Chinatown," which offered temporary freedom from abuse and their own form of social control and protection. It also offered some relief from drudgery, with the diversions provided by restaurants, the joss house (their house of worship), and gambling rooms.

In the Chinatowns of the western United States the population was predominately male, averaging twenty males to one female. Among Wyoming's 914 Chinese the ratio was forty to one. This tended to enhance the white population's notions of evils that existed in any Chinatown, including the one in Rock Springs. The census of 1880 did not provide a count of Chinese living in Rock Springs, but it did show that 497, more than half of those in Wyoming Territory, were in Sweetwater County. Because most of the Chinese in the county worked at the Rock Springs mines, it would appear that they accounted for at least one-half of the town's total population of 763. Clearly tensions were aggravated by the large influx of aliens that seemed to be "taking over the town." As the number of Chinese miners increased, the number of white miners remained nearly static. A Rock Springs newspaper, the *Independent*, probably reflected the perceptions of the white miners when it commented that while whites were being turned away from work, Chinese "were being shipped in by the car-load." It was frustrating and frustration often breeds violence.

Resentment among the whites was also aggravated by the refusal of the Chinese to join any labor union, including the fast growing Knights of Labor of the 1880s. The Knights, and most labor organizations, agitated for deporting the Chinese.

Rock Springs grew rapidly in the decade of the eighties and its population was probably well above one thousand by 1885, when the Union Pacific had five mines operating: Nos. 1, 3, 4, 5, and 6; No. 2 had been closed in 1883. During the summer of 1885 Union Pacific executives in Omaha and Boston were evidently confident of labor peace in Rock Springs since one wrote in a letter that some "matters of minor importance" would soon be settled. So it was with "utmost surprise," they said later, that they learned by telegram September 3 that "armed men . . . had driven all the Chinese miners . . . out of Rock Springs" and burned "some 50 houses owned by the company."

It all began with explosive suddenness September 2 in mine No. 6, on the west bank of Killpecker Creek north of the central coal camp and near the site of the original rock spring and stage station. An argument started between two white men and two Chinese over the right to dig coal out of a particular room of the mine. It quickly escalated into a fight that attracted men from adjoining rooms. More than twenty, about equally divided between the two factions, struggled and yelled in a blackness only partially penetrated by the flickering light from the miner's caps. Many caps were dislodged by blows delivered with picks, shovels and drills.

Someone must have raced up the manway to the mouth of the mine to spread word of the combat; Foreman James Evans hurried down into the mine, but by the time he arrived at the scene the fighting had stopped. The Chinese, carrying the seriously wounded, had started up the slope, and once out of the mine they disappeared into the houses of Chinatown or into huts near the No. 6 mine. Four of their injured were placed in a buckboard and hauled away; one of those later died. The white miners also left the mine and, walking south along the tracks of the mine's railroad spur, crossed Bitter Creek on the railroad bridge, and walked up to North Front Street where groups of excited men milled about until it was time to go home for lunch. Over the noon hour all saloons closed.

A mine boss, David G. Thomas, was standing on the No. 5 mine tipple that morning. Thomas had arrived in Rock Springs seventeen years before, when he was twenty-one years old, hoping the dry climate would repair damage to his lungs caused by more than ten years in the coal mines of Illinois, starting when he was ten. In Rock Springs he began as a mule driver in a U.P. mine, worked his way up to mine boss, studied law, and became friend and benefactor to many of the Chinese. This warm September morning from his vantage point on the No. 5 tipple he noticed unusual commotion about the town and soon learned its cause. He hurried to Chinatown, where he was known as Davy Tom, to advise the Chinese "it looks like trouble brewing," and he suggested they stay at home and out of sight. It was early afternoon when he was back on the No. 5 tipple and from there he could see what he later described as a mob with shotguns, rifles, and revolvers milling about at the railroad crossing near the center of town, from where they could look down on Chinatown. This mob of at least sixty white men, perhaps twice that, apparently decided, as the *Independent* reported the next day, that "John the Chinese must go," and, refusing to give the Chinese time to obey an order to leave, rushed upon the Chinatown huts, shouting, shooting, and looting.

A few of the Chinese chose to hide in their huts, but most fled in panic. Several were shot as they ran, a few fatally. Much of the firing appears to have been aimless, perhaps designed primarily to increase fright and flight. One eyewitness recalled seeing in the

51

attacking mob a woman with a revolver who "shut her eyes and turned her head every time she fired a shot, but she was making plenty of noise." Some Chinese slipped through to the west, but most ran to the east, where they tumbled down the north bank of Bitter Creek, scrambled through the mud of the bottom, and clawed their way up the south bank. From there, they scrambled over the railroad tracks and up the hillsides to temporary shelter in the sagebrush and greasewood of the ravines southeast of town.

After a few shots at the stragglers, the mob turned to scouring Chinatown, routing out and in some cases shooting those hidden there, searching for money and valuables, and eventually setting fire to every building. A number of the Chinese who chose to hide died in the flames.

Before the sun set beyond the ridge of White Mountain, a delegation had told James A. Evans, No. 6 mine foreman whom they believed favored the Chinese, to be on the next train east. Also threatened was W.H. O'Donnell, meat market operator who had been hired by the Union Pacific to be white "China boss," which meant principally that he helped the Chinese deal with the white system. Some of the rioters protested the threat to O'Donnell, because he was well liked. Nevertheless, he left town with Evans on an eastbound train that evening, but O'Donnell got off at Point of Rocks and returned to Rock Springs a few days later. Evans kept going east and never returned.

A Chinese clerk was hidden in the basement of the Beckwith-Quinn store for a week and one tale current in the town later asserted that a Mrs. Williams hid "a few" Chinese in the cellar of her house on M Street, but most of the estimated six hundred Chinese scrambled across the hills south of town and hurried west along the railroad tracks toward Green River. Some walked (or ran) the fifteen miles to Green River, but hundreds were picked up by U.P. trains and all were eventually taken to the Chinese colony in Evanston. A few hid in the hills for several days, getting food at ranches. Reports that as many as two dozen lost their way and died in the wasteland, some eaten by wolves, have never been confirmed. Sweetwater County Sheriff Joe Young arrived from Green River during the evening of September 2 and posted a few guards at mine and railroad properties, but he could not recruit enough deputies to fully restore law and order.

"All the night long," the *Independent* reported, "the sound of rifle and revolver was heard, and the surrounding hills were lit by the glare of burning houses." Next morning's scene was grim. A number of bodies were found in the smoldering wreckage.

Word of the carnage had reached Cheyenne on the day it happened. The territorial governor, Francis E. Warren, first telegraphed the army's Department of the Platte in Omaha, asking for military aid, and then the secretary of war in Washington, D.C., summarizing events and advising that the county sheriff had asked for military aid. The territory still had no militia.

Thursday, September 3, Warren was aboard a U.P. train headed west, and evidently he spent much of the time on the train composing a telegram to President Grover Cleveland. This telegram was sent from a Red Desert railroad station, seventy miles east of Rock Springs, known as Washakie, since renamed Wamsutter. He repeated the information sent to the secretary of war, but added: "Some forty houses burned. Three men known to be killed; many more believed to be. Mob now preventing some five hundred Chinamen from reaching food or shelter. . . . I believe immediate assistance imperative to preserve life and property."

After a stop in Rock Springs, Governor Warren went on by train to Evanston, where whites were threatening to repeat the Rock Springs "massacre" if Chinese employed in that area were not sent packing. From Evanston he wired President Cleveland again, warning of "open insurrection" in Rock Springs, where he now believed more than sixty had been killed.

Skeptical officials in Washington finally responded with military orders. About 7:00 A.M. Saturday, September 5, Companies B and E of the Seventh Infantry from Fort Steele arrived by special train to pitch tents on the west end of town and take up guard posts along the railroad.

The soldiers had been sent under orders "to prevent any interruption of the United States mails or the route over which they are carried," which, in effect, meant protect the Union Pacific.

Beyond that the troops were not to engage in local law enforcement. Maj. Gen. J.M. Schofield, commander of the army's Division of the Missouri, thought these orders inadequate. The railroad "is indispensible to the military service," he warned in a telegram to the War Department, and should be fully protected, including "those engaged in providing necessary fuel for the service of the road." That, obviously, would include several hundred Chinese at work in the coal mines in the Evanston area. Troops from Utah were sent to Evanston, where another riot seemed imminent, and from Fort Russell at Cheyenne the Department of the Platte sent an officer and ten men to Evanston with a Gatling gun, an early version of the machine gun. That same day Lt. Col. Henry L. Chipman, commander of the troops in Rock Springs, reported to the Department of the Platte headquarters in Omaha, "Everything upon the surface seems quiet."

Meanwhile, a coroner's jury impaneled in Green River found that eleven persons had burned to death in Rock Springs on September 2, and four had been shot "by parties unknown." Sheriff Young was not convinced the parties were unknown; he arrested sixteen at Rock Springs and jailed them at Green River, including Isaiah Whitehouse and William Jenkins, the two men who believed their room in the No. 6 mine had been usurped by two Chinese. Whitehouse was a newly elected Sweetwater County delegate to the territorial legislature.

Governor Warren was not satisfied. He wired Washington once more protesting that the Union Pacific "cannot enjoy the use and possession of its property unless troops assist the civil authority in making arrests in order to weed out all dangerous criminals and agitators and provide protection for reasonable employees."

Formal word of protest from another source had greater effect. The Chinese ambassador was demanding protection for the Chinese in Wyoming, and the federal government had no choice but to comply because such protection was specifically guaranteed in an 1880 treaty between the two nations. Finally, the troops at Rock Springs and Evanston were given orders essentially to keep

Infantry at parade rest on Rock Springs street after they arrived to keep the peace in September 1885.

Officers at Camp Pilot Butte barracks building in 1886. This building is the only structure of the military camp still standing, providing school rooms for the Catholic school. The officers were Lt. H.D. Styer, Twenty-first Infantry; Lt. William Stephenson, the post doctor; Lt. G.W. McIves, Seventh Infantry, and in background Capt. T.S. Kirland, Seventh Infantry. *National Archives.*

the peace, protect the mails and U.P. property, and protect the Chinese. On September 8 Warren was completing arrangements in Evanston to return the Chinese to Rock Springs by train with four companies of infantry following in a second train.

On September 9, at 4:00 P.M. the two trains arrived in Rock Springs with 606 Chinese aboard the first one; four companies of the Ninth and Twenty-first Infantry Regiments from Fort Douglas, Utah, aboard the second. These reinforcements for the troops already in Rock Springs were intended by the army "to render an attack on the Chinese at Rock Springs foolhardy in the extreme." The total number of troops in Rock Springs that night was about two hundred fifty. The Chinese were housed temporarily in boxcars parked on sidings near the mines, but carpenters hired by the railroad were soon at work constructing a new Chinatown on the site of the old. The carpenters had been hurriedly recruited by the Union Pacific from such places as Omaha and Salt Lake City. One who came from Salt Lake was the father of Edwin James of the Superior Lumber Company, who was to be mayor of Rock Springs from 1946 to 1957.

No mines were working in the tense town. If the Chinese were sent back to work, the company feared a walkout by engineers and supervisory crews, or a strike by all employees. In addition, the Chinese, understandably, were timid about reentering the mines. The Chinese boxcar homes were under military guard at night, but their occupants were free to wander about town during the day.

On September 15 two officials of the Union Pacific arrived and agreed to hear the grievances as voiced by an ad hoc committee of miners and merchants. On the seventeenth representatives of the government-appointed directors of the railroad, named to check on the activities of the Union Pacific, also sat to hear this committee. The grievances were basically these:

> Miners were cheated when coal was weighed.
> Chinese were employed before whites.
> Chinese miners were given the best rooms in the mines.
> The company sold privileges to the Chinese.

Whites were attacked in the mines by Chinese.

Miners were compelled to trade at the company store.

White women were unsafe because of the Chinese.

The evidence presented during the hearings was insufficient to substantiate these charges, although there had been incidents that seemed to justify some of them in the minds of the miners.

Simultaneously another inquiry was underway by agents sent from the Chinese consulates in San Francisco and New York. Their inquiry into who died in the attack on Chinatown was the most detailed, showing twenty-eight dead, all male, ranging in age from twenty-three to fifty-six. None had any family with him in Rock Springs except Leo Chih Mung, forty-nine, whose oldest son was with him and also worked in the mines. The son was not listed among the dead. The majority of the dead men had families in China. At least ten of the bodies or charred remains of bodies were found in burned wreckage of Chinatown dwellings. Why were so many caught in Chinatown? The consular agents learned that the Chinese miners thought the mob assembled that fateful day in "Whiteman's town" was just trying to scare them and would soon be dispersed by company officials. As a result few left their "huts" (the term used in the consular agents' report) until the actual shooting began.

A grand jury met to hear witnesses tell about the killing and destruction at Chinatown. It heard that the only Chinese woman there at the time was not hurt. However, David Thomas, who was thoroughly familiar with Chinatown, recalled two women living in Chinatown in 1885; one was the wife of So Qui, a "boss Chinaman," and the other the wife of a gambler who was seen carrying her across Bitter Creek as they fled to the hills. The grand jury also was told that some of the fires were set by the Chinese to save money and other valuables buried under their houses. The jury did not hear a single name of any person in the mob that attacked Chinatown. Although David Thomas did not testify before the grand jury, a comment he made years later about the events of September 1885, seems relevant. He said, "I was told to report for jury service in Green River and when D. O. Clark asked me why I did not want to serve, I replied that I did not feel that my back was bulletproof."

After some deliberation, the grand jury declared:

> We have diligently inquired into the occurrence at Rock Springs on the 2d day of September last, and though we have examined a large number of witnesses, no one has been able to testify to a single criminal act committed by any known white person on that day. Whatever crimes may have been committed there on the 2d day of September, the perpetrators thereof have not been disclosed by the evidence before us, and therefore, while we deeply regret the circumstances, we are wholly unable, acting under the obligation of our oaths, to return indictments. We have also inquired into the causes that led to the outbreak at Rock Springs. While we find no excuse for the crimes committed, there appears to be no doubt of abuses existing there that should have been promptly adjusted by the railroad company and its officers. If this had been done, the good name of our Territory would not have been stained by the terrible events of the 2d of September.

No one went on trial; all prisoners were freed.

A notice was posted at the Rock Springs mines announcing that mines 1, 3, 4, and 5 would open at 7:00 A.M. Monday, September 21, and that all men refusing to work would be discharged. About one hundred Chinese entered the mines that Monday; few whites showed up. Major General Schofield was in Rock Springs to observe, and September 22 he wired the War Department that he found the situation satisfactory.

On September 28 the report from the Rock Springs garrison was again all quiet, with the added footnote that eighty discharged miners had left town. The exodus had begun by those who had given up the struggle and decided to seek employment elsewhere.

As new housing was completed in Rock Springs, Chinese scurried back and forth between the boxcars on the siding and the new Chinatown, carrying bundles of belongings into the quarters they rented from the Union Pacific for $5.00 a month. They, like all U.P. employees, were also furnished with coal by the company for fifty cents a ton.

Since the all quiet reports from the temporary military posts at Rock Springs and Evanston continued into October, General Schofield ordered the garrisons cut, leaving two companies at Rock Springs and one at Evanston. The "Post Returns" from the Rock Springs military camp showed nine commissioned officers and 224 enlisted men present at the end of September. Only four officers and 91 enlisted men were listed at the end of October. Lieutenant Colonel Chipman reported the gradual exodus of the strikers was continuing and added that more white miners were returning to the mines. But despite these clear indications in October that the company had won, the soldiers stayed on and construction was started on permanent quarters for them. The Union Pacific provided land strategically situated between Chinatown and "Whiteman's Town" and some of the carpenters rebuilding Chinatown were reassigned to erecting barracks for enlisted men and quarters for officers on opposite sides of a small parade ground. The "temporary" military camp was officially named Camp Pilot Butte, a subpost of Fort Douglas, Utah.

The 1886 territorial legislature received a message from Governor Warren that reviewed the affair in Rock Springs and suggested that there was a need for "an organized territorial force" (militia) to back up the executive department in enforcing the laws. The legislators did not act on this suggestion, but neither did they respond to a request from House member Isaiah Whitehouse, a coal miner who took part in the original fight in No. 6 mine, for an inquiry into the use of troops at Rock Springs. Whitehouse also introduced a bill to require mine owners to credit miners with weight of coal mined before screening it to get rid of slack, rather than after. The legislature passed that bill but Governor Warren, calling it class legislation benefiting only one class of workers, vetoed it. The company-store policy was debated in the legislature, but a bill that would have banned withholding of wages to pay store bills was rejected. Approved were measures establishing the post of coal-mine inspector, prohibiting boys under fourteen and women from working in mines, requiring at least two openings to every mine and other ventilation and safety measures. An explosion at Almy (near Evanston) killed thirteen miners about the time the legislature opened its 1886 session. There is evidence that the law barring employment of boys in the coal mines was not enforced. Not long before he died, John Dickson told an interviewer he was taken into a mine to work with his father, Ross, before he was twelve; John was born in 1894.

The white coal miners' opinion that the Republican Warren was their enemy was reinforced by a news story in the *St. Louis Republican*. Warren was quoted as saying the men who committed "murder, arson, and robbery" in Rock Springs "were tramps and outlaws." The miners were, he said, "the dregs of the lowest order of immigrants, ignorant and brutal by nature." Because immigrants, English, Scotch, and Irish mostly, predominated among the white miners, it seems likely they predominated in the attacking mob, but the suggestion that these men were more brutish in their behavior than native-born American whites seems hardly credible.

The tragic affair in Rock Springs was not unique. A mob had attacked Denver's Chinatown in 1880, and more than twenty violent attacks on Chinese occurred on the West Coast, but the death toll was the greatest at Rock Springs.

By December the mine whistles were once again in control, inexorably dominating the schedule of life in the coal camp on Bitter Creek. Not much had changed, except the Chinese were an even larger proportion of the work force. December payrolls listed 457 Chinese at work in the Rock Springs mines and only 85 whites. Also the soldiers in ill-fitting dark blue wool uniforms and wide-brimmed, black felt hats were a constant reminder of the day disgrace was inflicted upon the town by what *Harper's Weekly*, a prestigious publication of the era, called "the utter fiendishness of a mob."

Camp Pilot Butte offered neither the best nor the worst of duty assignments for either enlisted men or officers. The officers eased their boredom by establishing a clubhouse open also to unmarried businessmen, coal department officials, and others of similar status. The club, located on B Street, was run by a black man and his wife under the direction of a steward, a post filled by rotation among the membership. The surgeon at Camp Pilot Butte

View looking north across Bitter Creek showing
footbridge over the creek in foreground, dugouts
along far bank, and Camp Pilot Butte in background.
Photo by H.H. Gibson. Sweetwater County Historical Museum.

for a few years, 1st Lt. William Stephenson, was the favorite club
steward because he managed to provide the most interesting
menus, perhaps the result of frequent hunting trips he made (with
the proper leave from post, the record shows).

The enlisted men were not generally regarded with approval
by the town's residents and seldom were invited into homes,
although there were a few marriages between Rock Springs
women and soldiers. The *New York Herald* described the soldiers of
the regular army as "poor shiftless waifs," compelled by
desperation or poverty to seek refuge in military service. The *New
York Sun* was less kind, referring to soldiers as "bummers, loafers,
and foreign paupers." Volunteering for army service, it was said,
was like volunteering for a penitentiary term—with one
difference: in the army you ran a much greater risk of being killed.
But not in Rock Springs in the 1880s. The Pilot Butte garrison
fired its Springfield rifles only on the target range, and that very
seldom.

Two views of Rock Springs taken about ten years apart. The top photo, taken in 1879, shows the No. 1 mine at right and the Beckwith-Quinn store far left. The No. 3 mine is in the background. *Sweetwater County Historical Museum.* The bottom photo shows the same section of town in the 1880s after Camp Pilot Butte was constructed (right of center). Just beyond the army camp are the shacks of Chinatown as rebuilt after the "massacre." *National Archives.*

The post routine was tedious from 5:30 reveille to taps at 8:15, and in no way brightened by fatigue details: policing the grounds, disposing of garbage, and filling the water barrels around the post, a particularly detested assignment during the winter. The food offered a matching monotony: beans, hardtack, bacon, coarse bread, beef hash or beef dried, occasionally a variety of wild game. Pay came every two months, unless the traveling paymaster encountered delays. A private received $13.00 dollars a month, in paper money, which was not always accepted by local tradesmen at face value, but the camp payroll undoubtedly had some impact on the town economy.

An 1881 order had prohibited sale of liquor at military posts, but it was ineffective, and in Rock Springs there were ample opportunities at the numerous saloons.

There were discipline problems, but no more than the average camp had. Some deserted; some were dishonorably discharged; a few were detained by civilian authorities now and then. A court-martial at Camp Pilot Butte in 1889 sentenced three men to four years' imprisonment for being AWOL. They were absent less than twelve hours and never strayed more than fifteen miles from camp. The case was cited by the *Kansas City Times* as an example of the excessively harsh punishments imposed by imperious officers. Adj. Gen. John C. Kelton wrote in his annual report of that same year that "too harsh and unequal punishments frighten many good soldiers into desertion." It was also true that many men, particularly recent immigrants, enlisted in the army with the intention of deserting once they had been furnished free transportation to the envisioned opportunities of the West.

On the whole the military played a relatively small role in the life of the coal camp, although the presence of the troops was seldom forgotten by the residents, both white and Chinese.

Engine at the Rock Springs station in 1881. The funnellike smokestack was designed to control sparking. *Sweetwater County Historical Museum.*

5

Coal Camp to Frontier Town

Soon after 1880 the population of Bitter Creek coal camp began to increase rapidly as the Union Pacific expanded its mining effort. Four U.P. mines were operating in 1884, and they accounted for most of the population increase, although some expansion in ranching contributed as well. It was clear the coal camp was struggling to become a town, and some people suggested the place needed organization, most importantly, an orderly layout of streets. In that year for the first time an engineer's survey gave legitimacy to the townsite, putting a stop to the helter-skelter settlement of the past with at least a semblance of a grid work of lots. Some buildings had to be torn down or moved because they were in the paths of the newly platted streets, but a few of the meandering pathways of the coal camp were simply converted into streets and never straightened out. The surviving famous (some might say infamous) K Street is an example. Today, the coal camp influence is also evident in South Front Street's long block east of C Street and very short block to the west. Felix Levesque, first U.P. agent at the Rock Springs station laid that area and when comment was made about the discrepancy between the size of the blocks, Felix was quoted as saying: "What's the difference? This will never be anything but a coal camp."

The haphazard placement of houses in the early years became a problem after formal property lot lines were established. For example: Joe Anselmi appealed to the city council for help when he discovered his house straddled a lot line and the owner of the lot next to his wanted to build. But if Joe moved his house over it would be crowding a house on the other side into the street.

Dozens of newcomers continued to arrive in Rock Springs with every immigrant train, despite the nationwide expressions of horror over the "massacre" of 1885. Between 1880 and 1890 the population of the coal camp multiplied four and one-half times from 763 to 3,406, and 60 percent of the total were immigrants.

Three exciting improvements in the last half of the decade enhanced pride in the town and faith in its future: Rock Springs acquired electricity, its first bank, and a water system. One man who visited Rock Springs with the idea of opening a bank was reported to have refused the opportunity after looking the place over. "Chinamen are too numerous and white men too few," he said, obviously influenced by the reputation the Chinese had for hiding wealth rather than banking it. But another banker, Augustine Kendall, representing investors from the town of Laramie who were looking for opportunities, learned that the railroad was building an electrical power plant and had plans to build a water pipeline from the Green River, thus eliminating two of the town's serious handicaps.

The power plant was constructed by the Union Pacific in 1886 to supply power to the coal mines, but it also sold power to the town and its residents and businesses. Power lines were erected along South Front Street and the lights turned on, for the first time, Christmas Eve, 1886. Some of the old kerosene street lamps, that had to be refilled and relighted one at a time every evening, were discarded. When the power lines eventually reached the houses on the north side there were some restrictions. In the houses it rented the Union Pacific permitted only one sixty-watt bulb in each room on a drop cord from the center of the ceiling.

A few months after the power plant was completed, Kendall and his partners had the Sweetwater Bank organized with a state charter and a capital of $25,000, doing business in a leased building that had formerly served as a butcher shop. The first depositors complained of the slaughterhouse odor, but that was eliminated when the bank moved; at the same time it was renamed as the First National Bank. (The former butcher shop served as the Navy Saloon for a time and then was leveled to make room for the Yellowstone Hotel.) Rock Springs National, the second bank, opened in 1892.

The Union Pacific constructed the water main from the Green River, using mostly laborers attracted from the Midwest by the offer of free transportation. One who accepted the offer was S.J. Sorensen of Omaha, who later said, "Best thing that ever happened to me," and stayed to make a home. The Union Pacific built the water system primarily to protect its property from the possible devastation of fire, but the townspeople knew that the end of the era of the daily water train and the hated water barrels was at least in sight when the pipeline was finished in 1888. Not every home had running water immediately. It was 1889 before the town had a contract with the Green River Water Works, a subsidiary of the Union Pacific. It took years longer to extend the mains into all parts of town. Many houses north of Bitter Creek were still using the odious water barrels after 1900. As the water and electricity lines came into the houses they rented from the Union Pacific, miners found new charges added to their bills when they appeared at the Beckwith-Quinn store at the first of the month to settle up accounts.

There was reason now for people of Rock Springs to believe they lived in something more than a coal camp, although the outdoor privies were still in every backyard. A sewage system, other than that provided by Bitter Creek, was yet to come. But they admired what urban-style amenities they did have, including not only the bank and a school, but two weekly newspapers—the *Independent* and the *Miner*, both founded in the 1880s.

In the autumn of 1888, three Rock Springs men asked the Sweetwater County commissioners to approve plans for incorporation of a town "to be named Rock Springs," covering two square miles, dissected by Bitter Creek, in township 19 north, range 105 west in the Territory of Wyoming. On October 6, 1888, the area described in the petition was incorporated, and November 13, 1888, the town elected its first mayor, W.H. O'Donnell, the meat market owner who was temporarily run out of town during the anti-Chinese riot. The *Miner* once rated O'Donnell "the most popular man in the county." He was a railroad worker near Rock Springs in 1868 when he was seventeen years old. Later he was

Rock Springs in the 1890s.
Map drawn by Frank E. Wright, adapted from an 1895 map by Paul C. Richards, Rock Springs city engineer, in collection of Sweetwater County Historical Museum.

hired as a clerk by the Wyoming Coal and Mining Company, and on an 1880 U.P. coal department payroll he was listed as a "China boss" paid $80.00 a month—the reason, no doubt, that some white miners perceived him as an enemy. He operated a meat market from 1882 until 1885, when it was absorbed by Beckwith-Quinn and he joined their staff. When Beckwith-Quinn went out of business in 1890, replaced by the Beckwith Commercial Company, Bill O'Donnell returned to the retail meat trade, opening the Central Market on South Front Street. Later he served as county commissioner and as county assessor.

Elected to the council were H.H. Edgar, Edward Thorpe, Augustine Kendall, and N.C. Peterson. Bill Mellor was persuaded to serve as town treasurer.

One of the first complaints the mayor and new council faced came from residents on the south side of the tracks who wanted relief from the stench of the slaughterhouse in their area. The council did order the establishment moved to a location a mile north of town, for "health reasons," the weekly *Miner* reported. The preferred residential section of the town was on the south side, and particularly along B Street. Here, for example, was the residence of Mr. and Mrs. Joseph Young, erected in 1888, with "an interior finished with elegant taste," the *Miner* said, and "furnishings most luxurious." Here also was erected the residence of Mr. and Mrs. John Hartney. He was a "Lanky" miner from England who abandoned the coal pits in the eighties to open a saloon on South Front Street—the ornately decorated Metropolitan near the depot—where his genial brother, Tom, soon joined him as a barroom greeter and host, and possibly bouncer. John Hartney's home, evidently because of the influence of Mrs. Hartney, was one of the first in town to have a lawn and flower beds. The *Miner* admiringly commented that "this sort of thing was extremely costly, all the watering having to be done with a hose attached to the water pipe." Such things were still news in a desert town emerging from coal-camp status.

As Rock Springs advanced into its third decade, now an officially recognized town, the territory advanced into statehood. President Harrison's signature on the statehood bill, July 10, 1890, ignited celebrations in Wyoming, particularly in Cheyenne, where Republican strength and statehood sentiment were both strong. One inspired orator there declared: "It means the dawning of a bright day, the beginning of an era of unparalleled prosperity.... A tide of immigration will set in. Capital will come."

Rock Springs, although not as enthusiastic about statehood as Cheyenne because of fear of increased taxation, managed at least one boom from a cannon, probably an artillery piece the troops at Camp Pilot Butte had been persuaded to load with powder. There is no evidence that any persons in Rock Springs believed the rosy words about a flood of immigration and capital. In fact, the 1890s brought hard times across the nation and to Wyoming. Prices and wages fell, businesses faltered. In the panic year of 1893, the Union Pacific Railway Company went bankrupt. Five years later it was reorganized in receivership as the Union Pacific Railroad Company under the management of Edward H. Harriman, tycoon and robber baron.

Despite the economic decline, Rock Springs continued to grow, but at a much slower pace. The population increase, most of it provided by the arrival of more immigrants from Europe, was only about a third of what it had been in the boom decade of the eighties. Even so the town's population increased by nearly one thousand during the nineties.

A number of civic improvements came about in the last years of the nineteenth century, including that symbol of culture so fondly desired by most western mining towns, an opera house, in which operas were rarely performed. Rock Springs' first opera house, seating five hundred, was built on the north side of the railroad tracks in 1889 by H.H. Edgar, lumber dealer and building contractor, and it was here road shows, traveling via the Union Pacific, performed. One of the first stage plays presented was *Uncle Tom's Cabin*. That opera house burned in December 1894. A replacement, "the pride of the city," had electric lights and steam heat and seated 750. The building also served as a public meeting house and dance hall. Community dances, featuring polkas, schottishes, waltzes, and square dancing, once held at Swanson's Hall, above the South Pass Saloon on North Front, or in a hall above the Fountain Saloon on South Front, could now be held on the opera house stage.

About 1890 the town had a volunteer fire department—twenty-four men known as the Clark Hose Company, named for the general superintendent of the U.P. coal department, D.O. Clark, who donated the man-drawn hose cart and five hundred feet of hose. The cart and hose were kept in a shed at Fifth and K Street; the fire alarm was the whistle at No. 1 mine. And in 1891 the residents were admiring a square, native-stone building of two stories on B Street—a new school of eight rooms! From there the first high school class of six was graduated in 1896.

Other improvements added were a state-supported hospital and a towered city hall. The hospital came about because the act of Congress admitting Wyoming as a state had set aside a land grant of 30,000 acres "for a hospital for miners who become disabled or incapacitated to labor while working in the mines of the state." The first state legislature authorized a general hospital to be located by popular vote at a city or town at which at least one thousand persons were employed as miners. The vote taken in 1892 selected Rock Springs. This miners' hospital was built at the south end of C Street, where the street reached the top of the hill near a favorite picnic ground, which had a great rock with a natural stairway children could use to climb to the top. The hospital opened October 1, 1894, and shortly after the *Miner* was complaining about the number of residents still going out of state for medical treatment. This first hospital building burned down in January 1897. While a replacement was being constructed patients were housed and cared for on the second floor of the brand new city hall. When the rebuilt hospital opened May 15, 1898, it was no longer the Wyoming State Miners Hospital but the Wyoming General Hospital, by new action of the legislature, which also declared it open to patients "of any society and class."

Fortunately for the hospital patients in 1897, the chief clerk in the coal company's office, William K. Lee, had been elected mayor in 1896. The city had earlier established a city hall building fund, but it was still inadequate until the newly elected Mayor Lee tossed in all the money paid the city for saloon licenses. Thus the

Original Rock Springs city hall built in 1897 was no longer in use in 1985. *Photo by Author.*

hall was completed in time to serve as a substitute hospital. It was built of sandstone quarried at a site two and one-half miles southwest of town. As a result the building closely matches the ecru coloring of the Bitter Creek landscape, which is dominated by grays and yellowish browns. Rather like a minor knight's medieval castle overlooking its feudal estate, the city hall towered over the town of 1897 in somber dignity. Its architecture has been described as "Richardsonian Romanesque" for its resemblance to the work of Henry Hobson Richardson, American architect who designed the Trinity Church in Boston.

Social events, such as dances, were frequently sponsored by the town's two dozen or more lodges and societies, including the White Mountain Court of the Ancient Order of Foresters; the Pride of Wyoming Castle of the Knights of the Golden Eagle; the Improved Order of Redmen, Washakie Tribe No. 5; and the Rock Springs Club, an association of business and professional men with what the *Miner* described as "cozy quarters" above the First National Bank. Various ethnic groups, such as the Scots, Danes, Finns, Slavs, and Tyrolians, also had their societies. The Andreas Hofer Society of the Tyrolians was an example. It was named for the great hero, an innkeeper's son, who led the Tyrolian peasants in rebellion against Bavaria in 1809. These societies collected dues from members to provide a fund to aid families stricken by illness, accident, or death. The common aid granted by the coal company to the family of a miner killed on the job in those days amounted to only fifty dollars. The ethnic societies attempted to supplement that. A member of the Andreas Hofer Society called at the homes of members to collect dues, ten cents every week, carefully recorded in a small notebook.

Among the males twenty-one years of age or older in Rock Springs, the foreign born outnumbered the native born by approximately five to one, and a heavy proportion of these men were single, living in boardinghouses or in "batches"—shacks or creek dugouts on the back of some other married miner's lot. The men in the batches usually boarded at the family home on the front of the lot.

A significant change in the make-up of the town's population of foreign born was taking place. The Chinese population had dropped, to less than three hundred, largely because of the effect of the Chinese exclusion acts barring further immigration of Chinese laborers; the first of those acts had been passed three years before the Chinese "massacre" occurred. In addition, the proportion of the foreign-born population from the British Isles and the Scandinavian countries was declining as the numbers of immigrants from eastern Europe (Austria, Germany, and Italy) rose. The census figures indicate that rare was the family in Rock Springs with two native-born parents who were both children of native Americans.

In the last two decades of the nineteenth century the number and variety of business establishments had increased dramatically. By 1903 Rock Springs had four general merchandise stores, three hotels, three restaurants, three drugstores, two banks, two meat markets, two barbers, two boot and shoe stores, a jeweler, a plumber, one cigar maker (Herman Lichtenstein), and thirty saloons!

The saloons were 40 percent of the commercial listings in a 1903 directory, and all were located on four streets: eight on South Front, seven on North Front, eight on wandering K, and seven on Pilot Butte. Three years later the editor of the weekly *Independent* estimated the number of saloons at "about 40," from which the license revenue amounted to only $12,000. The newspaper's editor urged a higher fee, high enough to reduce the number, thus freeing buildings for other kinds of enterprise. Wrote the editor, "a merchant coming to this city looking for a location finds but few." His plea had little impact; the saloon, a symbolic and ubiquitous institution of the Frontier West, remained long after the head of the U.S. Census Bureau declared in 1890 that the frontier line no longer existed. Nor did legislative efforts to curb saloons have much impact. The first Wyoming territorial legislature decreed in 1869 that saloons should close on Sundays; it had no appreciable effect.

So the saloons flourished, as well as the dance halls often associated with them and their back rooms with poker and other gambling tables. There were complaints about the noise of North

Front Street where music boxes at the Belmont Saloon and Dellapicola's dance hall played day and night. In the same area, only a few steps away, were the South Pass and the Senate saloons. The boisterous behavior that centered around the saloons occasionally escalated into violence, sometimes including gun play.

In 1891 at a barroom usually referred to as the Finnish saloon, the owner and one of his friends, after each had drained a number of glasses, decided upon a contest in pistol marksmanship. They drove a horse and buggy north of town to the area of the original rock spring and stage station where the No. 6 mine had been in operation from 1882 to 1886. There they decided their target would be a storage building. The first bullet fired at the building's door apparently missed; the second one, fired from a distance of about twelve feet, did not. It was followed instantly by a gigantic explosion that shook the entire camp. Bits of the two men, the horse, and the buggy were blasted as far as 300 yards; only a crater remained where the building once stood. It had been a powder house containing 1,213 kegs of black powder, 550 pounds of giant powder, and a supply of detonators. One house nearby was destroyed, several others damaged, one of which Thomas Crofts had just finished constructing. The Crofts, natives of Derbyshire, England, repaired their house and celebrated their sixtieth anniversary there in 1932.

The saloons, with their associated opportunities for diversion, attracted not only miners and ranch hands, but also the occasional drifters who followed the outlaw trail, which in one of its many versions included Rock Springs as a possible stopover point. This vaguely defined trail stretched diagonally across Wyoming from one infamous hideout, Brown's Hole or Park, about seventy-five miles southwest of Rock Springs, to another, the Hole in the Wall, near the southern tip of the Big Horn Mountains, southwest of Kaycee, Wyoming. Brown's Hole, a rugged but beautiful valley cut through the Uinta Mountains by the Green River, was a favorite spot of such outlaw crews as the Tip Gault Gang, the Tom Crowley Gang, the Diamond Mountain Gang, and the Rock Springs Gang. But the most famous of all was the Wild Bunch, led by Butch Cassidy (George LeRoy Parker).

Cassidy spent at least part of one winter in Rock Springs working in a butcher shop and in the process, according to some sources, acquiring the nickname of Butch. During his years as an outlaw around the turn of the century, Cassidy occasionally visited Rock Springs, sometimes to confer with his lawyer, who was reputed to be Douglas Preston, a highly respected member of the legal fraternity who later served as Wyoming attorney general and as district judge. Early in his career Preston established a reputation as a defense lawyer and at least once made a trip alone into Brown's Park to confer with one or more persons there who felt in need of defense. Another time he met with potential clients in the Boar's Tusk area north of Rock Springs. But need for defense was not enough for Preston; he also asked for reasonable and honest cause for the need. Perhaps his association with Cassidy began when they both lived in the Lander area.

Only a small part of the violence that tended to swirl around the saloons could be blamed on the outlaws when they came to town for supplies and diversions. In Rock Springs, despite its reputation as a melting pot of many cultures, there were occasional clashes between different ethnic groups, but cramped quarters in bachelors' huts, combined with drinking, probably triggered more. One night a fight broke out in a batch in the creek bed near No. 4 mine. One man died from a blow from a spike bar (normally used to remove spikes from rail ties in the mines), and another was stabbed but survived.

Violence was not confined to the towns of Wyoming in the decades spanning the turn of the century, but rather extended over the ranges where cattlemen battled homesteaders, rustlers, and the sheepmen. Cattle raising in the Rock Springs area never reached the magnitude it did in some other sections of Wyoming that had richer grasslands. However, enterprising early settlers in the high country around Rock Springs (elevation: 6,755 feet), where the rainfall averages a desertlike eight inches a year, soon discovered there were nutrients available, especially in the lowlands between the hills. The grasses, which grow in sparse clumps rather than in lush carpets, are thick-spike wheat grass, Sanberg blue grass, Indian rice grass, and needle-and-thread grass. In addition to the bush called Wyoming sagebrush there is the smaller and darker black sagebrush on the southern and western slopes. Also, black greasewood, with its cylinder type leaves and woody spines, grows three to four feet high in the flood plains, and two kinds of rabbitbrush flourish in these areas as well. Most important, in the bottom areas between hills, are the salt or white sage and the winterfat or Gardner saltbush, food for large herds of sheep that came to occupy the area around Rock Springs in the wintertime.

But in the Wyoming ranching boom that began about 1878 and extended into the eighties, the first ranchers in the Rock Springs area stocked cattle; later they learned the land was much more suitable for sheep.

The cattle boom had already begun to fade in the mid-eighties when blizzards of near hurricane force and blood-chilling cold struck during the winter of 1886-1887 decimating the Wyoming herds, many of which could get to neither food nor water during the storms. Problems for the big cattle ranches were made worse by annoying competition for the land from small ranchers and farmers. Disputes over use of the public lands for grazing and the struggle to curb rustling culminated in the "Johnson County war" in north-central Wyoming when an invading force of ranchers and their hired gunmen killed two men they believed to be cattle thieves.

After that scandalous episode the influence of the cattle barons began to decline, but violence on the range did not, because after the disaster caused by the winter of 1886-1887 many ranchers had turned to raising sheep. While the cattlemen who persevered were struggling to survive, the sheepmen, according to Thomas Moonlight, Wyoming territorial governor at the time, were "happy, buoyant, and hopeful." Tim Kinney and others in the Rock Springs area were among those who made the switch. To curb the advance of the sheep herds onto the most desirable ranges, some cattlemen turned to violence again, resulting in what has been called "the range war," which lasted until 1909.

Some of the early incidents in this conflict occurred on the ranges south of Rock Springs where the cattlemen of northwest

Colorado and the sheepmen of southwest Wyoming clashed. The sheepmen drove flocks, sometimes as large as two thousand sheep, across the line into Colorado for summer grazing on the free public lands that the cattlemen wanted for their herds. According to one account, the Edwards brothers, Welshmen from Rock Springs, were the sheepmen most hated in Colorado. In 1895 the cowmen of Routt County, Colorado, warned Wyoming sheepmen to keep out, but the conflict continued until November 10, 1899, when a sheep camp forty miles northwest of Craig, Colorado, just a few miles south of the Wyoming border, was attacked by masked riders. The next year Colorado cowboys were patrolling the state line in an effort to keep the sheep out.

Nearly three million sheep were grazing the Wyoming ranges by 1900, each flock in the charge of a single herder with a couple of dogs. Many of the flocks wintered amid the sheltering sagebrush and greasewood in the hollows between the hills around Rock Springs or on the Red Desert to the northeast, not merely surviving but thriving on the salt sage. But the sheepmen wanted their stock moved to the grasslands for the summer, and this almost inevitably meant the public lands the cattlemen claimed by right of previous use. The cattlemen announced that the New Fork country of the Green River Valley, north of Rock Springs, was out-of-bounds for sheep, and in July 1902, when fifteen herds of sheep belonging to Rock Springs sheepmen crossed the deadline to get into this area, some of the sheep camps were attacked by a reported 150 masked men. One herder and at least 2,000 sheep were killed.

These and other incidents around the state helped prompt the sheepmen to organize the Wyoming Wool Growers Association. John Hay, Sr. of Rock Springs was the vice president of this group of only forty sheepmen who found themselves largely helpless in a struggle with the powerful Wyoming Stock Growers Association, which had been in existence for more than twenty-five years, was controlled by the cattlemen, and whose will, as one historian put it, was law in Wyoming.

Less than a year after the wool growers association was formed, a sheepherder from a Utah ranch was killed at a sheep camp in southwest Wyoming, another case of a cattlemen's deadline ignored. In April 1909, about the time that the Wyoming Wool Growers announced their membership had reached 541, fifteen masked riders killed two prominent woolgrowers and a herder near Tensleep on the eastern edge of the Big Horn Basin. Five men were sent to the penitentiary with sentences ranging from three years to life for what became known as the "Tensleep raid," and the range war was ended.

While the war raged over the range, there was relative peace between labor and management at the coal mines. There were more deaths in the mines than there were on the ranges, but the mine deaths resulted from accidents. However, no major mine disasters occurred in the Rock Springs district.

Two major improvements in mining equipment were initiated in Rock Springs before 1900. In the 1880s the U.P. Coal Company installed the first air-operated cutting and drilling machines in the No. 4 mine. About ten years later came the first step in mechanized hauling: an electric mine locomotive, the first ever built in the United States, went to work in U.P. No. 7 mine at Rock Springs. The squat little engine hummed up and down the slope of the mine, tugging trains of loaded cars up and coasting down with empties, except when it took the "man trip," cars carrying miners. It was quickly dubbed "Charlie Smith," for its first driver, and when it was ceremoniously "retired" in 1929, it was inducted into the Union Pacific Coal Company's Old Timers Association and mounted on a pedestal in front of the Old Timers building.

Before the turn of the century a number of companies besides the Union Pacific tried coal mining in the Rock Springs district, and those that achieved some degree of success appeared to have the blessing, in one way or another, of the Union Pacific. When Congress passed the Sherman Antitrust act in 1890, monopoly practices and restraint of trade were barred, so independent coal operations could no longer be squelched by refusing them rail service. Two of the most successful independent mines were opened by former employees of the Union Pacific. About two miles south of old Blairtown, in a draw cut by a now-and-then stream that drained into Bitter Creek, Mark Hopkins opened up a mine in

Union Pacific's No. 1 mine in a photo taken by J.E. Stimson of Cheyenne, date not known. *Sweetwater County Historical Museum.*

1888, and the camp that sprouted there was called Hopkinsville. Hopkins, who was a delegate to the convention that drafted a Wyoming state constitution in 1889, was on the U.P. Coal Company "time roll" for 1887 as "assistant general superintendent" at a salary of $250 a month. Within a year after opening his mine, Hopkins sold out to the Central Coal and Coke Company, and the name of the camp was changed to Sweetwater.

Central also took over a mine nearby at a camp called Quealy, named for a former U.P. mine superintendent. A native of Ireland, Patrick J. Quealy as a child came to the United States with his parents and was working in a Missouri mine at the age of nine. He worked for the U.P. Coal Company for several years and served briefly as inspector of coal mines in Wyoming Territory before he organized the Rock Springs Coal Company, evidently with the knowledge and approval of the Union Pacific. In addition to opening the Quealy mine that Central took over, the Rock Springs Coal Company leased and reopened the old coal mines at Blairtown. These too Central bought, so after 1910 the only non-U.P. mines in the Rock Springs area for several years were operated by Central Coal and Coke.

Chinese were still employed by the U.P. Coal Company, but they were a diminishing proportion of the Rock Springs work force. Their processions to the mines in the morning and home again at night were part of the daily ritual in Rock Springs. They marched to and from the mines in groups, each group proceeding in single file, keeping a conversation alive by relaying comments back and forth along the line.

The Chinese cemetery was located to the north of town on some relatively flat ground between two hills, an area that can be reached today by Community Park Drive. Services for the dead were held in Chinatown, and then the bodies were taken to the cemetery for temporary burial, under about three feet of the sandy, rocky ground, because it was always the plan that the bones would eventually be sent back to China for permanent burial there. It was the Chinese custom to place freshly prepared food on the grave. After the mourners had departed, white youngsters, who often made a sport of teasing the Chinese, would come racing down from a nearby hilltop hideout and make off with the food, frequently sweet and sour pork or roasted duck, coconut sticks, lechee nuts, or chocolate candies. Many of the bones were subsequently disinterred, cleaned, then sealed in airtight cans and shipped to China; the cemetery was eventually abandoned.

Every February the Chinese attracted great attention when, in celebration of their new year, they staged the annual parade of the dragon. The monstrous dragon, elegantly fashioned of green silk and paper and festooned with mirrors, was variously reported to be 70 feet long up to 130 feet long, carried by 30, 50, or even 100 men. It may be that there were actually two different dragons in Rock Springs at different times. One of them was reportedly purchased in San Francisco and brought to Rock Springs by the town's best known Chinaman, Lao Ah Say. Ah Say had first arrived in San Francisco in 1857, worked in the goldfields for a

Dragon on parade during celebration of Chinese New Year in Rock Springs. *Sweetwater County Historical Museum.*

time, and then was hired, with his partner, Ah Koon, by the Central Pacific Railroad to manage its large crew of Chinese track builders. After the railroad was completed, Ah Say lived in Evanston, Wyoming, until he was hired to help recruit and "boss" Chinese laborers for the U.P. mines at Rock Springs.

Ah Say, usually dressed in an American-style suit and cane in hand, marched at the head of the dragon parade, followed by persons carrying poles festooned with exploding firecrackers. Next came the "teaser," a man carrying a bamboo pole with two multicolored banners used to irritate the dragon, make it more ferocious in destroying devils and other evil spirits that might be lurking about the town. As the dragon, head tossing and smoke pouring from its nostrils, writhed its way through the streets, stopping frequently to posture and threaten before some house that might contain evil spirits to be exorcised, it was followed by men in Chinese costume carrying battle axes, spears, and swords and by others exploding firecrackers or beating on gongs. The din was considerable.

Ah Say was at one time believed to be quite wealthy, although before he died in 1898 he had apparently fallen into stringent economic times, perhaps partly because he had spent lavishly on entertaining others. When Chinatown was no more and the area it occupied incorporated within the town, one new street, about two blocks long, was named Ahsay Avenue.

Another leading Chinese resident was the proud and loyal Lao Chee, a native of Canton, widely known in Rock Springs as "Jim," "Doctor Jim," or "Jimmo." He started work in the Rock Springs mines in 1880, survived the "massacre" in 1885 by fleeing to Green River, and thirteen years later was appointed stable boss at the main U.P. Coal Company stable located near the present Pilot Butte Avenue bridge over Bitter Creek. There he conscientiously tended about two hundred horses and mules, often talking to them in a wonderful mixture of words from many languages, accumulated from his numerous friends in the polyglot town. He wore a special policeman's badge and revolver, granted him by the mayor to help him deal with tramps who liked to sleep in the hayloft. He also assumed the task of chasing the kids from the streets at curfew.

All but a few of the Chinese were still living in Chinatown, with Camp Pilot Butte solidly entrenched between them and the white town to the south. There seemed little reason to believe that the soldiers would ever have to hold off another attack on Chinatown, but they stayed on, performing "the usual duties of the post," as the monthly reports to the Department of the Platte headquarters phrased it. Rumors occasionally seem to have swept through the town that the army planned to end its "occupation" of Rock Springs. The Chinese became so concerned by such a rumor in June 1891 that they drafted and signed a petition to the War Department requesting that notice be given well in advance of any plan to transfer the soldiers so the Chinese might "make preparations for moving to a place of safety." Fifty-seven of the signatures on the petition were identified as those of miners, forty-eight others as names of laborers (in handwriting that was strikingly similar), seven of merchants, and three of "China bosses." There were no plans to move the troops, the War Department replied.

Chinatown's guardian troops at Camp Pilot Butte by the 1890s had a fairly extensive and reasonably comfortable post. In addition to the barracks building and the officers quarters, there were corrals, stables, chicken house, wagon shed, carpenter shop, gun shed, barber shop, ice house, beer cellar, canteen, bakery, commissary, hospital, schoolhouse, and guard house.

Cross-country marches and target practice were fairly regular activities; sometimes detachments camped for a month at the target practice range, which for a time at least was a seventeen-mile march away at a place called Sweeney's Canyon. The camp garrison generally numbered about 60 enlisted men and three officers with an exchange of troops occurring with Fort Douglas, Fort Russell, or Fort Logan once or twice a year until late in 1894 when monthly exchanges of about 25 men began with Fort Russell in what was apparently a training effort. After the United States declared war on Spain in April 1898, the garrison soon dropped to one officer, a second lieutenant, and 17 enlisted men. Six months later 106 men of the Twenty-fourth Infantry arrived for training, and practice marches became a regular Saturday event.

The final post return from Camp Pilot Butte was dated February 28, 1899, and reported 50 men of the Twenty-fourth Infantry still there. A hand written comment under "Record of Events" read, "The filthy condition of the immediate neighborhood of the post in the Town of Rock Springs is apt to cause sickness later in spring when ground thaws." This comment, possibly written by or on the orders of the commanding officer, 1st Lt. George McMaster, might have been prompted in particular by the condition of Bitter Creek. Whether this comment hastened the army's decision to abandon Camp Pilot Butte is not known. The last soldiers left in March. Camp Pilot Butte's guardian role, which obviously had not been needed for some time, was finally ended.

6

The Company Town

The scrawled complaint on the last Camp Pilot Butte post return form, dated 1899, about the health danger posed by Bitter Creek might have been an unintended prophecy of what was to come about eighteen months later. The yellowing and brittle pages of old ledgers in which early burials were recorded at Rock Springs show an alarming number of deaths attributed to typhoid fever in the late summer and fall of 1900. In addition to "tiford fever," as it was often spelled in the burial records, other feared killers were "brown caties" (bronchitis) and diptheria. Was there a link between the sicknesses and the malodorous pollution in the creek or, perhaps, the stagnate water barrels still in use at many households?

Or could there have been a problem with what flowed from the pipes of the much-admired water system? The system had shortcomings, such as inadequate pressure all-year round, frozen fireplugs in the winter, and muddy water in the spring. Morris Hardware on South Front was advertising a filter "to save you from water that is thick with mud to settle on your kidneys." The dispute between town and waterworks, owned and operated by the Union Pacific, continued until 1916 when the Wyoming Public Service Commission ordered lower rates, filtering, and higher pressure.

Not much was being done, however, about disposal of the town's sewage. But one strong voice of "boosterism" in Rock Springs was not discouraged. When the outspoken editorialist Bill Barlow of the Douglas, Wyoming, *Budget*, declared Rock Springs "notoriously unclean and unattractive," James E. Hill, editor and proprietor of the Rock Springs *Independent*, marshaled the following counterattack in his issue dated June 17, 1905.

> It is a well known fact that Rock Springs is one of the cleanest towns in the state. One man and a team are employed constantly in cleaning the town and hauling away the dirt as fast as it accumulates and another man is hauling gravel with a team filling in the sunken spots about town, while the third man and team are at work sprinkling the streets and when not at work sprinkling, is also hauling gravel. Our gutters are all stone in the business portion of the town and the residence portion of the town is being attended to in the same manner, while a number of stone crossings are laid about and more are being prepared. Altogether Rock Springs is a neat up-to-date town, with a wide-awake mayor and council and outsiders, especially newspapers, should not knock us.

Even the "boosterism" of James Hill failed the test when it came to Bitter Creek in midsummer. In the *Independent* dated July 28, 1905, he wrote:

> The town is in good sanitary condition with the one exception of Bitter Creek. The odors that greet the nostrils of the passersby are frightful and if we have an epidemic of typhoid, or other fevers in the city, there will be no doubt as to the cause. The creek is a hard proposition to deal with, in fact the only remedy is a sewage system and the sooner the system is contracted for and in use the sooner the danger of an epidemic is passed.

"Sooner" for Rock Springs in the matter of a sewer system was another decade away. The malodorous and possibly sickening effluvium was largely created when residents cleaned out backyard chicken coops or pens and barns where cows and horses were kept. This manure as well as trash, such as cans and bottles, was dumped into the creek channel. Lacking indoor facilities, many folks also had their outhouses located on the banks or in the channel of Bitter Creek.

The creek was just one of the pestering problems left over from the days of the coal camp. Complaints about livestock roaming the streets unattended and eating produce from wagons left loaded overnight for early morning deliveries prompted the city council to establish a pound for unfenced critters. Two other problems the coal camp bequeathed the town were not so easily solved. The first business buildings and homes had been erected on both sides of the tracks and directly over the mines. Then the Union Pacific built its main switching yard parallel to its main line through the center of town, eight parallel sets of tracks running east and west between the two Front streets. A few hundred yards west another switching yard of a half-dozen tracks running north and south divided the original town plat from the first addition known as West Flat. Single tracks stretched like tentacles through the town, connecting these two main yards with the coal mines.

This network of rails formed barriers to movement about the town, and getting across the eight sets of tracks between South and North Front was particularly inconvenient and hazardous. For about the first fifteen years of Rock Springs' history there were two approved crossings from north to south, one at C Street and the other at K Street, but when the Union Pacific built a new depot and loading platform where K Street reached the south side of the tracks, the K Street crossing was closed. As a substitute, the railroad constructed a viaduct, for pedestrians only. This massive steel structure, high enough for the largest locomotives to go under, became part of the town's skyline, a major civic eyesore some thought, with a red light on the top; when the light was on it was a signal to patrolmen to phone city hall to learn where they were needed. Children loved to stand on the viaduct directly above a passing train so that the huge puffs of smoke and steam enveloped and warmed them as it flowed up through the cracks of the walkway. This viaduct was only slightly less offensive, some said, than the gigantic black coal chutes for replenishing the hoppers of the locomotives. The chutes loomed on the horizon about one hundred yards east of the viaduct.

By 1912 the single crossing for vehicles at C Street, which pedestrians also often used, no longer seemed adequate. With the switching of freight and coal cars, passenger trains parked at the depot, or freight trains parked while locomotives took on coal and

South end of the viaduct for pedestrians to get across the tracks was located a few yards east of the depot. This viaduct was torn down when the underpass at C Street was built. *U.P. Railroad Photo, County Historical Museum.*

water, the crossing was frequently closed, sometimes for fifteen or twenty minutes, backing up traffic on both sides. An appeal to the railroad to reestablish the K Street crossing was rejected because of the cost of rearranging the depot and other facilities. Things would remain as they were, except the Union Pacific redesigned the north stairway access to the viaduct to provide room for widening North Front Street.

The Union Pacific did eventually agree to try to hold the periods when C Street was blocked to five minutes, and it constructed a tower from which a guard could lower gates to block the crossing when he spotted approaching trains or switch engines. Later a warning signal was added, a gong that started a loud clanging when a train approached.

Adults as well as youngsters frequently walked along the tracks to get from one section of town to another and just as frequently took shortcuts across the tracks on errands or on the way to school, even crawling under parked freight or coal cars when necessary. Sometimes those cars were hooked to switch engines that moved suddenly without warning. In the period from 1910 to 1915 at least six persons were killed on the tracks—three boys, two men, and one seventy-seven-year-old woman who was picking up coal along the tracks at the coal chutes, a practice that someone engaged in almost daily. Often several men who needed money picked mushrooms along the tracks and sold them to housewives, who cooked them with a silver dime; if the dime turned green, the mushrooms were thrown out.

Excavations in the coal bed underneath the town were a threat as well; cave-ins left gaping holes in streets and threatened to swallow whole buildings. One occurred near the hospital and another just east of the southside Catholic church. Considerable consternation resulted November 29, 1916, when a section of North Front Street in front of the Grand Opera House suddenly dropped into an entry or worked-out room of the No. 1 mine, leaving a hole fifteen feet in diameter and forty feet deep. The city had it filled with rock and dirt.

There was another major topic for talk of the town in the first decade of the twentieth century when word got around that organizers for a new union were quietly talking to local miners. The United Mine Workers of America (the soon to be familiar UMW) had been founded in Columbus, Ohio, in 1890 but started organizational efforts in Wyoming only after 1900. After establishing a local union in the northern Wyoming coalfield of Sheridan County, the organizers arrived in Rock Springs. Very little appeared in the newspapers about this, but it is clear that the mine owners, led by the Union Pacific Coal Company and using the full clout of the railroad, vigorously opposed the union, even for a brief period carrying out a threat to close the mines. It also became clear during this confrontation between management and labor that the Union Pacific had deliberately followed a policy of recruiting miners from various countries abroad on the theory

"Hot Weather Sale" at Rasmussen's Department Store in 1911.

that it would be difficult to form a united front with men who spoke a wide variety of languages and little or no English.

Despite the possibilities that they might be locked out of the mines and evicted from the houses they rented from the Union Pacific, a large number of miners signed up with the UMW. When it became clear that the union had won this opening struggle, the U.P. Coal Company, in an impressive display of good sense, turned its end of the negotiating over to Morgan Griffiths, a Welshman who came to the United States in the early seventies, worked his way across the continent as a miner, joined the Knights of Labor, and arrived in Rock Springs in 1879. He quickly rose to supervisory positions and in 1907 was the general underground foreman for the Union Pacific Coal Company in Rock Springs. He was trusted by the miners and talked their language. A general agreement was reached, and the mines were soon back at work producing coal at a record rate to meet a record demand.

That agreement with the UMW, signed on September 1, 1907, was statewide and included a clause establishing the eight-hour day in Wyoming's coal mines. When the agreement expired one year later, the coal companies proposed a reduction in wages. The UMW promptly called a nationwide strike, and more than two thousand miners in the Rock Springs area walked out. Many miners grasped the opportunity to return to Europe for a visit, others turned their attention to planning a Labor Day celebration for September 7, 1908, which turned out to be windy and dusty. That Labor Day, a mule named Maud, pulling a load of coal, won the prize for the "most comical" parade entry; quoits were played in front of the Union Hall, and, as inevitable as oratory at any Rock Springs holiday celebration, there were foot races, including a potato race, a wheelbarrow race, and a baseball game; the town team, playing a team from Cheyenne, lost for the first time that summer.

During the strike families had extra time for picnics either at the rock near the hospital or, if they had transportation by horse and buggy or a hired stagecoach, at one of two out-of-town spots: Kent's Ranch south of town, or Six Mile, on the road north. Rock Springs could be largely depopulated on summer Sundays if the

A section of K Street about 1910. The bridge spanned a part of Bitter Creek that was eliminated in a rechanneling project in the 1920s. *Sweetwater County Historical Museum.*

At the C Street crossing and South Front Street in the early 1900s. *Sweetwater County Historical Museum.*

Swedes were picnicking at Kent's Ranch, the Finns at Green River, and there was a baseball game at Green River as well. A favorite pastime on summer evenings, when the air cooled quickly, was to sit outside watching the flames of bonfires young folks built on the top of No. 5 hill northwest of town.

When the strike was settled before the end of September and the mines reopened, the top wage in Rock Springs became $3.40 for an eight-hour day. That was in a period when a nickel would buy a six-ounce glass of beer; lunch to go with it, at most saloons, was free. Nickel beer had come to Rock Springs in the 1890s when Joe Avanzini opened a new beer parlor and cut the price of a foaming glass from ten cents to five. The other bars followed suit and from then on Avanzini was known as "Five-cent Joe."

The years spanning the turn of the century were a time of relatively high demand for coal and this spurred renewed prospecting in southwestern Wyoming and greater production in the existing mines. The Union Pacific was not the only coal producer in the Rock Springs area. At the Sweetwater mines a camp of about one thousand persons had been established. Some workers commuted to Sweetwater from Rock Springs, a few of them making a ten-mile round trip on foot, carrying a tall, round, aluminum lunch pail with three compartments: in the bottom compartment was water, tea, coffee, or sometimes wine, the weak "third" wine made from a batch of grapes; a meal was in each of the other two sections, because the miner was often in the mine long enough to need two meals. At 4:00 or 5:00 A.M. each day the women prepared the meals and packed the lunch buckets as they cooked a large breakfast, not only for their husbands but often for one or more bachelor boarders.

The Central Coal and Coke Company was still operating its mines at the southeast edge of Rock Springs, and new mines had been opened at Black Buttes by the Rock Springs-Gibraltar Coal Company and at Gunn-Quealy, about four miles northeast of Rock Springs by the Rainbow Rock Springs Coal Company, P.J. Quealy, president.

The Union Pacific was operating five mines in Rock Springs: No. 1 (the only mine in number one coal seam), and Nos. 7, 8, 9, and 10, all on the number seven seam. (The two Central Coal and Coke mines were also on the seven seam.) The U.P. company was also out prospecting because of increased demand and also because it was about ready to close down historic No. 1. The working face of this great producer was now so far underground that the hauling costs were troubling management. The U.P.'s prospectors had taken a look at most of its land grant, and at additional potential coal land it had acquired by using "dummies," persons who bought the land from the government and then transferred it to the coal company. That practice, engaged in by a number of coal companies, was uncovered by the federal government and the land was restored to the public domain through legal action.

Prospecting results led the Union Pacific to open a mine near the east edge of the Rock Springs uplift and about twenty miles northeast of Rock Springs. When the railroad got a spur line up Horsethief Canyon to this area, production was started in 1906, at a coal camp called Superior. But miners were reluctant to move into the barren hills to a camp that had no road, only the rail line for one train that left Rock Springs about 7:00 A.M. with empty coal cars and returned in the evening with loaded cars. Coupled behind the coal cars would be a baggage car for hauling mail, produce, and other food; also, various items of freight needed by the Superior camp; then, at the very end, was a passenger car. It was called the "P and P train," for "pigs and people, pigs first."

Getting cash to Superior safely on paydays was also a problem. E.P. Philbrick, known as Broncho Jim, was an agent for the company at the time. He volunteered to carry the pay satchel to Superior and persuaded those in charge at the central office to let him handle it alone. After dark he set out on horseback with the satchel, riding north a few miles then east over the hills to Superior, returning the same night. He did this several times before the secret got out, then the method of transporting the pay satchel had to change.

In July 1910 old No. 1 was finally closed after the Union Pacific had opened another new mine seven miles north. Employee housing was quickly erected, and trains from Rock Springs brought water in tank cars to this place called Reliance until well drillers finally managed to tap an underground pool of potable water at a depth of 115 feet. Reliance soon had its own school, a town band, a dance orchestra, and occasional local talent entertainments.

People from the outlying camps frequently came to Rock Springs for shopping and entertainment, which could include shows by traveling troupes that came through on the railroad and stopped for one-night stands at the Grand Opera House, later renamed the Union Opera House when the unions acquired the building on North Front. The bookings during the period included Wagner's opera *Parsifal,* and plays entitled *The Girl and the Stampede, Wizard of Wall Street,* and *Why Girls Leave Home.* Prize fights now and then and the balls of the bartenders and firemen were held at the Grand. Beginning in 1907 there was another choice for entertainment at a new theater called the Empire on Pilot Butte, which was showing "moving pictures." Another alternative on a Sunday in June was to attend "the zoo," the big picnic at Green River sponsored jointly by the Elks, Owls, and Eagles. In 1908 the Rock Springs train station sold 500 round-trip tickets to Green River for the Sunday of the zoo picnic.

The Searchlight and the Caledonia clubs were two social groups largely confined to residents of the south side of town, although residence there was not a requirement for membership. The name Searchlight was clearly intended to convey a sense of the purpose of that club: searching out knowledge. Its meetings usually emphasized papers prepared and read by members on various topics, often rather ambitious in scope, such as "Mexico, Its Early History." Roll call was answered by briefly reporting on some event of current interest. One meeting was held at the bottom of U.P. mine No. 4, with permission of the coal company. The program, appropriately, concerned coal. The Caledonian Club was for people of Scottish descent. Its principal event annually was the celebration of the birthday of the Scottish poet, Robert Burns, in January. At one of these parties, a dinner held at the Elks Club, a major item on the menu was "trummlin wullie" (head cheese).

Increased employment in the area brought increased prosperity for the saloons and brothels, of which the most notorious in the first two decades of the twentieth century was "the white house on the hill," sometimes referred to as "the white house" or, even more briefly, as "the hill." This bordello was a white-painted wood structure located southeast of the main section of town, and about halfway up No. 1 hill, so called because the No. 1 mine was at its base. Prominently visible from the town below, the white house was only a short buggy or horseback ride away, about where the present streets of Edgar and Liberty intersect. James Hill crusaded against the white house and its "painted fairies" in his weekly *Independent* over a period of several weeks in 1906 while he was also fulminating about the restaurants in town that were circumventing the law, he thought, in serving wine to women customers. It would all be a "disgrace to hell itself," he wrote, pointing out that a city ordinance had been passed closing all the "wine rooms" in town and barring women from saloons. That ordinance was one of the few successes of the reform element, which lost its major journalistic mouthpiece in 1907 when Hill suspended the *Independent*. A few months later C. Lou and Cora B. Wanamaker purchased Hill's printing equipment to send up, they said, "a rocket" from the banks of Bitter Creek, the first issue dated November 27, 1907, of a new weekly they called the *Rocket*. Despite its name, the *Rocket* never matched the crusading zeal occasionally exhibited by Hill's *Independent*.

A reform movement called the Citizen's Ticket promised a city administration free of saloon control in the election of 1910, but the majority of the voters, as they had in most previous elections, supported a Republican ticket. John H. Anderson, popularly known as Jack, was elected mayor in that year and reelected each year following until 1916. He might have modeled his life after a hero in any one of the more than one hundred novels penned by Horatio Alger, Jr. during the last decades of the nineteenth century. Like the Alger heroes, Anderson, depending almost entirely upon self-reliance and exemplary endeavor, conquered poverty and other assorted handicaps to rise to wealth and position. Anderson was born in Scotland but came to the United States with his parents when he was six years old. He arrived in Rock Springs in 1883 with eighteen cents as his total capital, according to one newspaper article, and worked for eight years digging coal and driving a mine mule. Then he became a delivery wagon driver for local stores until (as so often happened in the Alger stories), a local capitalist recognized his sterling qualities. In Anderson's case the capitalist, a fellow known by the improbable name of Count Von Knoblock, manager of the Wyoming Beer Company, made Anderson the driver of his delivery wagon. In a few years Anderson succeeded Von Knoblock as head of the company. To distinguish him from two other Jack Andersons in town, he was known as Beer Jack. Compounding the confusion, the other two Jack Andersons were saloon keepers, but since one was distinctly larger than the other, he was Big Jack and the other was Little Jack.

Once every year during his five years as mayor, Beer Jack reverted to his one-time role as delivery-wagon driver when with the $500 he was paid each year for being mayor, he bought and delivered on Christmas Eve a fat turkey to each of the neediest families; the needy Chinamen each got a fat pig.

The dispute with the Union Pacific over the need for reopening the K Street crossing arose during Anderson's term as mayor. Not much could be done by mayor and councilmen in the way of land use without consultation with and approval from the railroad, the majority property owner. When citizens asked Mayor Anderson and his council to approve a new street they were told the city officials would have to check with the U.P. Another delegation proposed a park in the No. 4 district; Mayor Anderson would have "to see Mr. Manly." Frank L. Manly was superintendent for the U.P. Coal Company. This was not timidity on the part of the mayor and council; it was recognition of a fact of life in Rock Springs.

The relationship between the town and the Union Pacific Railroad and its subsidiary companies was an uneasy one that swung like a pendulum between angry conflict and friendly cooperation. Without the company the town would not exist; but the town wanted freedom to grow up and make decisions on its own. When push came to shove, however, the company's will usually prevailed. Periods of worry about rumors that the U.P.

Coal chutes near the center of town; there was a track
on the right as well as the two in the center. The figure
near the center appears to be that of a woman
gathering lumps of coal. *Sweetwater County Historical
Museum.*

Coal Company might be closing down were not infrequent, and
that did eventually happen.

Unquestionably the Union Pacific had clout not only in Rock
Springs, but in Wyoming generally, but usually it tried to use this
influence sparingly and circumspectly. Nevertheless, there were
many who believed the company was managing elected officials
like puppets.

While the town council faced problems posed by railroad
tracks on the surface of the land and mine excavations below it, the
school board sought ways to provide up-to-date equipment for
instruction and adequate space for increasing enrollments. The
board did manage to provide two Remington typewriters for the
high school, one brand new. In the main school building on B
Street many of the desks intended for one pupil were being used

simultaneously by two. Part of the burgeoning enrollment was caused by an increasing number of pupils staying in school beyond the sixth grade. The teachers also reported another problem: "the oversizes"—youngsters who were beyond the normal age for classes in which they were enrolled. These problems were discussed at the annual school district meetings held every spring in one of the town assembly halls or theaters. School board members were also elected at these meetings.

By 1911 the town had a new elementary school on the north side and small schools at No. 4, No. 6, and West Flat, with the overflow at the City Hall and a rented former Finnish church. Even so, by 1912 there was a waiting list for first grade.

On the last day of January 1916, "a day of joy," the *Rocket* reported, the crunch was relieved when students moved into another native-stone building on B Street, a new $80,000 high school. With its domestic science and manual training rooms, science laboratories, sanitary drinking fountains, and gymnasium with separate showers for boys and girls, this building was the town's latest pride. In 1916 the schools enrolled 1,899, including 219 in the high school, which then included the eighth grade.

As the general population of the town grew, reaching 5,800 in 1910, the number of Chinese dwindled until, in 1913, the famous dragon could not march in the new year parade; the few dozen Chinese survivors, mostly elderly, were inadequate for the task of carrying it. The dragon was sorrowfully destroyed. Repatriation and death were the major factors in the decline of Chinatown; with increasing frequency the town watched as a single file of fewer and fewer shuffling mourners followed the horse-drawn hearse from the mortuary on K Street to the Chinese cemetery. Each new grave was still carefully provided with food for the departed's journey to another life, food which the children of Rock Springs continued to pilfer as soon as the cortege disappeared back down the gulch. The Union Pacific divided the Chinatown area into lots for sale, after reserving two small blocks for the use of the remnants of the Chinese colony and enough for a school playground at North Side Elementary, later renamed Washington School. That decision offered the schoolchildren a diversion during recess that no one had planned on: digging for souvenirs dropped or discarded by the former Chinese occupants of the land.

The dusty, unpaved streets constituted one of the problems the mayors and the councils faced. These streets were the major source of the dusty film that covered almost everything in Rock Springs much of the time. The fretful and seemingly interminable winds drove the dust and the fine, gritty sand through the cracks somehow, even if windows and doors were kept tightly closed. One could wake up in the morning to find miniature sand dunes on the sill of a closed bedroom window. Of course, in the winter, the windowsill might be covered with miniature snowdrifts instead. The sprinkling wagon controlled the blowing clouds of dust only part of the time on the most traveled routes; housewives in the less affluent residential sections got little help in dealing with the dust.

The sidewalks—where they existed at all—were still mostly boardwalks and often in need of repair. Deteriorating boardwalks of the downtown area had become an issue before Beer Jack was elected mayor, and in the summer of 1908 the broken and treacherous boards along South Front were torn up and replaced by cement. About a month later the *Rocket* proclaimed "most joyful news," cement walks were to be extended to C and B streets and to North Front. Construction of cement sidewalks continued into 1912 with property owners paying the costs, and no record of protest from the town's biggest property owner, the Union Pacific. The town would be known, the *Rocket* now predicted, "as the city of good walks."

But the streets, alternately dusty or muddy, were still a problem. A test section of paving was laid from the railroad tracks south along C Street to the city hall in 1915; unfortunately that one block of pavement was all Rock Springs had to admire for several years. The suspicion in town was that the Union Pacific had quietly informed the city administration that the company would not support an expensive paving program, which would have to be paid by property assessments. As a substitute each year for about a decade the town observed a "street day" when most stores closed, and volunteers turned out with shovels, rakes, wagons, and trucks to haul, spread, and roll cinders on the streets to provide a smoother, although temporary, surface. Those found not participating ran the risk of a fine at a kangaroo court.

Adding to the pressure for street improvements was the arrival in Rock Springs about 1908 of one of the wonders of the age—the automobile. Joe Iredale, Rock Springs' postmaster during the first decade of the twentieth century, built one of the first autos in town, and another was constructed by Fire Chief John Forndran using buggy wheels. Dr. R. Harvey Reed bought a factory-made electric model; when the batteries ran down he hired a team of horses to tow it to the U.P. powerhouse to have the cells recharged. W.J. Kellogg of the Rock Springs Lumber company had a Model T Ford painted, according to the newspapers, a bright red; but that must have been the result of Kellogg's own hand because all the Model Ts of that era came from the factory in one color, black. Mayor Anderson and John Hay, rancher-banker, acquired autos, too; Anderson's was a steam-driven Franklin with its own electric-lighting plant; Hay's was a sleek Pierce-Arrow. John Hay was the president of the Rock Springs section of the National Highway Association, whose principal objective was getting the Overland Trail declared the route for the transcontinental highway.

Improvements could not come fast enough for the auto enthusiasts. The stretch of road from Rock Springs to Point of Rocks was particularly bad, under water two feet deep at times, washed away by cloudbursts at others, extremely rough and dusty when dry. One early auto tourist found the answer; he loaded his car on a train at Wamsutter, unloaded it at Rock Springs.

In 1913 the Lincoln Highway was officially proclaimed for a route paralleling (and for a number of miles actually using) the original railroad bed across southern Wyoming. In celebration of the triumph, Wyoming Governor Joseph Carey proclaimed October 31 a day for "old time jollification," with bonfires, general rejoicing, and Sunday sermons on the life and ideals of the man for whom the highway-to-be was named, Abraham Lincoln.

The routine of life in the coal town, where the 1910 census counted nearly six thousand persons, was hardly affected. In

Panoramic view of Rock Springs in 1915 from No. 5 hill (now called College Hill) looking southeast. Beyond the creek in foreground are the houses of West Flat where Christian Bunning and family lived. In background (from left) are Chinatown, Camp Pilot Butte, North Front Street, No. 1 mine, South Front Street, city hall, the two-story stone school building on B Street, and (far right) the hospital at the top of C street. *Photo by J.E. Stimson of Cheyenne. Copy provided by Sweetwater County Historical Museum.*

summer, women watched for delivery wagons of the Wyoming Beer Company, Krug Beer Company, or Bunning Transfer bringing ice from the West Flat sheds where it was stored in sawdust after winter-time harvests on the Green River. Wagons (sleighs when there was enough snow in the wintertime) from the various mercantile stores also made daily tours from house to house for the driver to take orders. In the afternoon or the next day they retraced their routes to deliver the groceries or clothing. But that did not always meet the needs of the women of the Rock Springs households. People who lived there as youngsters remember almost daily trips to the stores on foot. Sometimes more than one trip a day was required, to butcher, to baker, to grocer, and when the man of the house returned from the mine

near day's end, there was often another trip to be made, carrying a five- or ten-pound lard pail, to Pa's favorite saloon where the pail was filled with cold beer. In the summer, the youngster was nearly always reminded that the return trip this time must be made on the shady side of the street.

Stores on the north side included the Finn Store on M Street and the larger Union Merc and Miners Merc, which both offered free delivery, even to homes as far away as Reliance. They also had to offer credit to compete with another major market on the north side, the company store, now owned outright by the U.P. Coal Company. Beckwith-Quinn, after it lost its role as company store, sold out to its last manager, A.F. Neuber, who took in a partner and changed the store's name to Beeman and Neuber Mercantile Company. Beeman and Neuber was one of the two major outlets patronized principally by the business and professional leaders and their families on the south side. The other south side store was Stockgrowers, which was originally rancher Tim Kinney's store, later owned cooperatively by a number of ranchers.

The stores continued their free order-taking and delivery system long after telephones were available because some customers refused to use the newfangled gadget; it didn't work well anyway, and few of the working class homes had them. Many immigrant housewives had enough trouble with the English language, without trying to speak it over a telephone. Phone service improved in 1913 when a new system made one- and two-party lines possible, but then patrons had to "call by number" because the operators at the switchboard were no longer familiar with all the names. A similar evidence of progress had occurred in 1909 when free mail delivery was established with three carriers. Residents then had been warned that house numbers had become essential. But Rock Springs habits died slowly, or not at all; long time residents, even into the 1980s, have persisted in giving directions not by street and house number, but by landmarks, "Well, you know where Mrs. Tyler lives..." Or "You know where the library is ..."

The library had become a principal landmark after it was built on C Street in 1908. It was one of more than twenty-eight thousand made possible by donations from Andrew Carnegie, Scottish born magnate who made millions in steel manufacturing. Mrs. Mary A. Clark gave up teaching to become the first librarian. For nearly thirty years she ruled the storehouse of books from her desk near the entrance, passing out library cards, squelching any rowdiness, checking out books. Sometimes she vetoed selections made by children if she thought choices inappropriate; there was no appeal. The library was a popular spot on Mondays; children went there to read the Sunday funnies in the Denver and Salt Lake City newspapers. But some youngsters, intimidated by the librarian's reputation, never entered the place.

The town was plagued by too many freely roaming dogs. Action of the city council in establishing a $3.00 license fee did not seem to reduce the canine population. The dogs even wandered in and out of the theaters at will, sometimes getting into fights in the aisles or between the seats. Finally the two theater managers, D.T. Gilmore at the Oracle and Thomas Berta at the Grand, announced that "no dogs of any size will be admitted ... no exceptions."

7

The Melting Pot

When Queen Elizabeth II visited the United States in 1984 she sought out surviving evidence of the British influence in Wyoming, and she found it, among other places, near Sheridan at the Bradford Brinton ranch house, now a handsome museum perserving the quality of the grand baronial life style of the British ranchers in Wyoming in the nineteenth century. That life style had little in common with the struggle for survival of the coal miners in grimy dugouts on Bitter Creek—except many of the miners were also British. For evidence of the role some Britons played on the mining frontier for territorial Wyoming the queen might have visited Rock Springs, the outcome of a coal camp that was established almost exclusively by her countrymen more than a century before her visit. The Blairs were from Scotland; the Wardells were from northern England; Bill Mellor, who helped locate the No. 1 mine and was its first superintendent, was from Lancashire, and most of the men who dug the coal also came from the British Isles.

In 1870 the population at the Rock Springs coal camp and at Blairtown was 117, of whom 74 (63 percent) were immigrants, mostly from Great Britain. When this tiny colony amid the Wyoming sagebrush had expanded to 3,406 by the census of 1890, the foreign born (2,033) still accounted for 60 percent of the total. In the Wyoming population as a whole in 1890 the foreign born amounted to only 24 percent.

A breakdown by countries of origin of the foreign born in Rock Springs was not given in the census of 1890, but it was provided for Sweetwater County, and Rock Springs contained 70 percent of the county population and 80 percent of the foreign born. The figures for the county show that the nearly 1,200 persons from Great Britain and Ireland accounted for about 85 percent of the foreign-born whites. About 500 of the remaining foreign born in the county were Chinese. The English, Scots, Welsh, and Irish continued to dominate Rock Springs until well into the twentieth century, filling nearly every supervisory position in the coal company and most of the municipal offices after the town was organized. That preeminence tended to continue even after their numbers were no longer predominant because they had advantages in seniority, in previous experience with the mining system, and in the dominant language of the camp.

Despite this Rock Springs did not become a tiny British "colony," but rather it soon became noted for its remarkable mixture of ethnic backgrounds. The coal company, although overwhelmingly British-dominated, was the major influence in introducing diversity. Wardell broke the first strike in 1871 by bringing in Scandinavians. There were 264 Scandinavian-born residents in Sweetwater County in 1890. When the U.P. coal department faced another walkout in 1875, its answer was to import the Chinese.

Through the 1880s Britons continued to arrive in approximately equal numbers with other nationalities, principally Scandinavians and Germans, including German-Russians, but during the following decade the flow from Britain ebbed as the tide from the eastern and southern areas of Europe began to swell, the beginning of what has been called the "new immigration." After 1890 the new immigration became a flood. How this affected Sweetwater County and Rock Springs showed up in the census of 1900. That time about 1,000 natives of the British Isles were counted and nearly 1,500 from six other countries of Europe, significantly including Austria and Italy.

Many of the first to leave a European village or region were persuaded to do so by agents of the U.S. companies, including the Union Pacific. Then letters home from these early arrivals, telling of employment opportunities in such places as Rock Springs, persuaded others to follow. Thus people from the same village in

Europe often settled in the same town in the United States. So they came from Italy, Greece, Czechoslovakia, Rumania, Hungary, Yugoslavia, Austria, Germany, and Russia. They were not afraid of hard work; in fact many came with the sojourner's objective: to work hard enough to accumulate some of the wealth of this fabulous land where fortunes flowered so readily to return to the homeland able to buy new comforts. They did find that hard work won better rewards in America than it had in Europe, and, in the frontier society of Rock Springs, they also found it won them unexpected status as free members of an egalitarian society where they could call the boss by his first name. These were among the reasons they decided to stay.

The new immigrant flood continued through most of the first two decades of the twentieth century, and the 1920 census figures show that foreign-born white persons accounted for 13 percent of the total population in Wyoming; by contrast, foreign-born whites were 33 percent of the population in Rock Springs, and the figure was almost exactly the same for all of Sweetwater County. The foreign born in the county that year included 928 from Great Britain and Ireland, somewhat less than the count had been twenty years earlier. The British in Sweetwater County were now outnumbered more than three to one by the more than 3,000 from European countries, and the overwhelming majority of those had come from southern and eastern Europe. Major numbers were recorded in Sweetwater County in 1920 for Austria, 300; Greece, 445; Yugoslavia, 685; and Italy, 723. Those few who had somehow found their way to Rock Springs before 1900 had served as magnets, drawing their relatives and friends. They came for greater economic opportunity, for freedom from oppression, or for freedom from the threat of war. Immigration from southern and eastern Europe was encouraged by coal companies, which no longer sought the skilled miners from Britain because the mechanization of the mines was well under way, so unskilled labor would now do, at considerably lower wage cost.

The country of origin given for immigrants was not always an accurate indication of the ethnic background involved or of the immigrant's own view of his or her nationality. Many from Russia were in fact Germans who had first migrated to Russia but had become dissatisfied there. Others of the "Russians" were in fact Poles; but because the nation of Poland did not exist before World War I many who came from that divided region were counted as Russians, Germans, or Austrians.

Another group, the Tyroleans, left the Alpine villages of the Dolomite Mountains before 1914. Should they be counted as Austrians or Italians? Many of those people always insisted they were Austrian, which was true, because they came to America before World War I, when their villages were within the borders of Austria. After that war their villages were incorporated into Italy as part of the spoils of victory. Often, however, an immigrant from the Tyrol simply said, "I'm Tyrolean." There seemed to be more pride in that for them than in being either Austrian or Italian.

Immigrants often felt lingering attachment not to a nation they had departed, but to a province, or simply to a valley or town. Many of the Tyroleans in the Rock Springs district came from the Val di Non, a small picturesque valley hidden behind a range of the Dolomite Mountains west of the much-traveled route from northern Italy to the famous Brenner Pass. Their language, despite some vocabulary and inflections peculiar to their valley, resembled the dialect spoken widely in the Trentino-Alto Adige region of northern Italy.

Among the first to come to Rock Springs from the Val di Non were Peter Prevedel, Olivo Anselmi, Joseph Anselmi, and August Menghini from the village of Brez; and Pete Genetti of Castelfondo; and Frederico (known in America as Henry) Bertagnolli of Tret (Fondo). These and other early adventurers wrote letters home that helped trigger a major exodus from the Trentino region between 1901 and 1913, part of it to Brazil and Argentina in South America and part to the United States. When World War I brought a halt to this migration the Rock Springs area had one of the major Tyrolean settlements in the United States, with a favorite gathering spot at the Fountain Club, a saloon on South Front Street, only a few steps from the depot and often the first stop for many new arrivals from the Tyrol. One estimate indicated there were one thousand Tyrolians in Rock Springs in 1911, including nearly one hundred families from Brez. The men came first, often with the intent of making lots of money working in the mines and then returning to the Tyrol, but, typically, most found themselves better off in America and decided to stay. Money saved was instead sent to wives or sweethearts to pay their passage. Many of the Tyroleans soon learned that the opportunities for "upward mobility" characteristic of the American frontier were still available in Rock Springs. They emulated the Britons and others; the men leaving the mines, the women stepping out beyond the home, to become citizens of influence in business and community affairs; their children, often college graduates, advanced even further in business, professions, and politics.

Henry Bertagnolli, who was in Rock Springs at the time of the Chinese "massacre" but took no part in it, quit the mines to establish a livery stable, which he soon expanded. In the early 1900s, with investment help from relatives and other fellow Tyrolians, the store added hardware, clothing, and groceries. Thus that small Bertagnolli store became the Union Mercantile Company, a favorite of many for nearly eighty years, and one of the largest general merchandise stores in Rock Springs.

Joseph Anselmi left Brez for America in 1895 when he was eighteen years old. He apparently had been recruited to work in a coal mine at Cambria, in northeastern Wyoming, but he stayed there only a few years before moving to Rock Springs. He sent back for a bride, Maria Menghini, and they were married in Rock Springs in May 1903. Joe left the mines to work in the U.P. store and bakery, which provided the training that made it possible for him to form, with a group of friends, the Pilot Butte Grocery, which soon became the Miners Mercantile Company. Both the Union Merc and the Miners Merc offered items, especially food, of interest to Tyroleans, including polenta flour, a coarse grind of cornmeal that was still popular in Rock Springs in 1986, but by that time only available at a store established by Ben Boschetto, son of another Tyrolean immigrant.

In the same years that Tyroleans were leaving their villages, another exodus of similar proportion was taking place from villages in a mountainous region of Slovenia, also before World War I a part of Austria, later awarded to Yugoslavia. These immigrants probably accounted for a large part of those Rock Springs residents counted in the 1920 census as Yugoslavians. Slavs from a wide region of Europe flooded into America between 1900 and 1914; among the more than one hundred thousand arriving in the United States in 1906 was Mary Zaversnik, a native of a small Slovenian village near Ljubljana. After a year's anxious waiting, Mary had received money and a summons to join her husband in America. Setting out alone on a journey whose hazards she could only guess at, she probably traveled north across Austria and Germany to the port of Bremen, where most of the Slavs embarked to cross the North Sea and Atlantic Ocean to New York City.

For most immigrants the experience of leaving their native villages and traveling halfway around the world was made terrifying by a feeling of helplessness—finding one's way to the right road, the right ship, the right train from gestures, often given impatiently, by strangers; surviving a succession of innkeepers, boatmen, customs agents, and frontier guards; protecting one's purse from toll gatekeepers, cheats, and pickpockets. But for Mary at least the sea voyage in a steel-hull ocean liner lacked the hazards and discomforts that had characterized similar journeys in wooden sailing ships in the previous century. But another ordeal began after she had been disembarked into the maelstrom of Ellis Island, where immigrants were "processed," some rejected. She neither spoke or understood English, but in that, of course, she was not unique.

Mary had some help from Slavic benevolent societies whose members offered guidance to new arrivals. Someone pinned on her coat a tag with her name and destination: "Rock Springs, Wyoming," words with little meaning for Mary; she couldn't even pronounce them. But that tag helped her get on the right train out of New York, helped her make the correct change of train at Chicago, and, miracle of all miracles, got her off the train safely in Rock Springs. There, like many before her, she found her home was a dugout huddled against the bank of Bitter Creek. Each successive wave of immigrants found shelter in the dugouts that earlier arrivals abandoned as soon as they could afford better. Eventually Mary and her husband, Anton, and their children also moved up, literally, to a house in the No. 4 district.

They were allowed to buy a small lot from the U.P. Railroad on a bench of land newly made a part of Rock Springs, and there they built a house above ground, except for the washroom in the basement, a house with modern plumbing, a house with many windows!

When residents of Rock Springs total up the "nationalities" or ethnic groups that have shared the history of the city, they may come up with forty, or 50, even as many as sixty, depending on criteria used. The number is not important, except as it may lend greater emphasis to the view that Rock Springs represents the success of that part of the American dream called "the melting pot."

Rock Springs probably has as good a claim as any community in the United States to the title of melting pot, but not all who came found it possible to fit it. The obvious example, of course, is provided by the Chinese, but even immigrants from Europe often found it difficult to adjust to American society or to be fully accepted. The women particularly tended to cling for psychological support to the language and the ways of the old country. It was a traumatic thing to be torn away from family and friends, from the familiar village square where one got the news of the day while doing the laundry at the public fountain, and from a way of life developed through centuries of experience.

New arrivals in Rock Springs took housing wherever they could find it, but preferably near persons who spoke their language. Many Tyroleans lived for years on or near M Street; some of their descendants still do. However, in years prior to World War I, the residents in the M Street district also included Spanish, Finnish, French, Greeks, English, Italians, Germans, Welsh, Swedish, Norwegians, and Slovenians. In Rock Springs company housing encouraged mixing and discouraged ethnic neighborhoods, not because of company policy, but simply as a matter of housing availability. There was never a Little Italy or Little Austria in Rock Springs, although there was for a time Chinatown.

Mary Zaversnik found that many of her neighbors in the No. 4 district were Slovene, but just as many were not. As the nine Zaversnik children grew up they, like the children of other immigrants, far outstripped their parents in the Americanization process because they were unrestrained by any social system brought from Europe. They adapted to—or rather simply accepted—a childhood world in which their friends and playmates had last names such as Blackledge, Buh, Blakely, Bozner, Armstrong, Bosnick, and Furmon (the last the name of a family of blacks). It never occurred to them that there was anything unusual about this. As soon as the children were old enough to go to school the Americanization process was accelerated. Room 1 at the first school in the No. 4 district had more than sixty first graders in 1908; all but a half-dozen used a language other than English at home. At school only English was spoken and the teachers, strict disciplinarians, insisted all children, no matter their age, learn English to grow up to be "good Americans." Immigrant parents, generally, supported the teachers, in fact insisted upon an almost holy respect for them. The Rock Springs school system before World War I attempted to accelerate the process for adults as well by offering "Americanization" classes each winter, including instruction in the English language and in U.S. history and government.

There were no real barriers to being accepted in Rock Springs, although the social life of those to whom English was a native language tended to be separate, at least in part. Until well into the twentieth century this division corresponded, very roughly, with the division between the north and south sides of the tracks. The laborers lived on the north; the professional people, mine supervisory personnel and business people, for the most part, lived on the south. There was a feeling, undefined and rarely talked about, that the two areas, separated by the tracks, were different. For youngsters it was mostly a friendly rivalry; for north side students their contemporaries at the Yellowstone

Elementary School on C Street (south side) were "yellow bellies," while south side students pretended scorn for the "wash tubs" at Washington School on Ahsay Avenue (north side). However, class lines on the frontier, and Rock Springs in 1915 still had many of the characteristics of a frontier town, were not firm; they were easily breached. When children from both sides of town enrolled at the only high school, situated on the south side, the assumed distinctions seemed to disappear.

Was Rock Springs, then, the melting pot in action? Many writers and speakers, most of them immigrants, attempted to define the concept of the melting pot. One who had major influence, perhaps, was Israel Zangwill, an English author who was never an immigrant himself. In his melodrama called *The Melting Pot* the United States was depicted as a fiery crucible that purified the immigrant strains and fused them into a super-race: "Americans." At Henry Ford's factory in Detroit this concept was illustrated during a pageant that employees enacted as part of their Americanization instruction. During this performance a column of immigrants, dressed in a variety of old-world costumes, filed from one end of the stage into one side of a giant pot, while another line emerged on the other side all dressed alike, American-style, and waving the Stars and Stripes. This symbolism suggested that the true melting pot would boil out differences, all vestiges of foreign culture. That view of the melting pot seems to have been more than just implied in 1948 by Eugene McAuliffe, then president of the Union Pacific Coal Company, when he said:

> A quarter century ago it still was possible to gather any one of a number of national groups who were proud to entertain their friends with their old national folk songs, music, and dances. Time has changed all that. A half grapefruit, with ham and eggs for breakfast, together with white bread in ample quantity, coupled with the democracy afforded by association in the public schools and on the playing fields, have brought about almost complete elimination of sharp racial characteristics that tended to separate peoples.

The hall on Bridger Avenue the Slavic societies built and where grape festivals and other community celebrations have often been held. *Sweetwater County Historical Museum.*

Slovenes with costumes and handiwork displayed during the International Night celebrations. Those identified in this photo are Mary Mrak, Mrs. Matt Ferlic, Mrs. Anton Oblok, Mrs. F. Fortuna, Mrs. Mary Galicich, and Mrs. J. Yugovich. *Sweetwater County Historical Museum.*

That was not a popular view in Rock Springs, which had for years supported the preservation of a variety of ethnic characteristics, not the elimination of them.

Rock Springs applauded the cooperative effort of the Slav lodges and benevolent societies in building the Slovenski Dom for a meeting house, which they shared so fully with the population at large that it became a community social hall. It has served many purposes, but none more popular than as the location of the annual harvest festival, an event that featured performances in native costume by a number of ethnic groups, many but not all of Slavic origin. The festival also featured dancing, mostly the polka. At the Dom on festival nights one might sample a variety of marvelous foods, such as *kranski koblasi* (sausage still highly admired in Rock Springs), *flancita*, and *potica* (pronounced poh-TEE-sah), a rich nut spread rolled and baked in a delightful dough.

Rock Springs massively supported International Night, the variety show featuring hometown talent, that was initiated and sponsored for a few years by the Lions Club. This show played to standing-room-only crowds, dramatizing multi-ethnic aspects of the town with music, dances, foods, and a display of arts and crafts.

When the Danish brotherhood scheduled its annual picnic at Kent's ranch, south of town, in the years before World War I, a near majority of the townfolk attended—and were welcomed. Finnish summer outings at Green River were just as popular, again for all nationalities.

The Rock Springs concept of the melting pot was not the homogenized blending of a variety of cultures, or a fusion of many old cultures into a single new one, the sort of thing Ford and Zangwill found inspiring. The people of Rock Springs recognized that they had a harmony of imported cultures, and they chose to celebrate their differences. The mixture made for an ethnic and cultural richness that is still present in Rock Springs. What Rock Springs had developed was, in the sociologist's terminology, a pluralistic society, one which not only tolerated diverse groups but valued them, yet also supported a common social order. This seemed to work well in Rock Springs, where there were no major clashes between ethnic groups, with the single exception of the attack on Chinatown in 1885, and neither did the groups live apart in ghettos, as distrusted, even feared, strangers to each other.

It may be significant that Rock Springs was born after the Civil War, which scoured away antiimmigrant sentiments of the 1850s. The Union armies enlisted 500,000 foreign born, and immediately after the war foreigners helped build the U.P. railroad and provided vital labor in other areas, including the coal mines. But the antiimmigrant movement or nativism returned under the pressure of the economic depression in the 1890s, particularly with the anti-Catholic American Protective Association. Three state legislatures petitioned Congress to call a halt to the "invasion" from Europe. One—Wyoming's—declared that indiscriminate immigration was threatening to overwhelm the nation. None of this nativism seems to have had any impact in Rock Springs.

World War I, however, provided a major test of the ties that the aliens and newly naturalized in Rock Springs had for the United States. As it turned out, those ties stretched a bit, but they did not break. As the war in Europe began in 1914 the future looked comfortably promising for Rock Springs with a surprisingly strong surge in the demand for coal. The U.P. Coal Company's payroll increased significantly as traffic on the railroad increased, and independent producers found an apparently insatiable market for their coal. One miner was quoted as saying, "People would buy anything, as long as it came out of the ground and was black."

This demand for coal was one of the repercussions in the United States caused by events in Europe. A powder keg of nationalistic rivalries had exploded into war with the assassination of an Austrian archduke in Sarejevo, Serbia, an area south of Slovenia. U.S. industry frantically geared up to help satisfy Europe's appetite for enormous quantities of ammunition and other war materiel. Coal was needed for the factories producing the materiel and for the railroads called upon to move it. Consumption of coal by the U.P. railroad increased dramatically; the road's locomotives burned 1,342,000 tons in 1916, up 15 percent from the previous year. Coal consumption for heating also soared as constant winds swept the high country during weeks of bitter cold. Then the trains, which had been coming through Rock Springs at the rate of more than one an hour, suddenly were not coming at all. During the last week of January 1917 snow was added to the wind. The blizzard piled up snowdrifts so deep forty-five trains were reported stalled for sixty hours on the Wyoming division.

As the heavy train traffic resumed in February, the railroad announced that the total output of the seven U.P. coal mines in the Rock Springs area, about ten thousand tons a day, would henceforth be reserved for exclusive use of the railroad; the mines had been selling about one thousand tons a day on the commercial market. The Gunn-Quealy Coal Company pushed up production at Sweetwater, south of Rock Springs, and a firm from Denver, the Colony Coal Company, opened a mine to the north where it built a camp of one hundred homes called Dines.

After the United States entered World War I in April 1917, even more and longer coal trains were loading and whistling and switching about in Rock Springs. Through traffic soared to an average of fifty trains a day, twenty-five each way. It seemed like the C Street track crossing at the center of town was blocked more hours each day than it was open. Frustrated residents fretted, but the *Rocket* softly reminded them that "we must bear it with patience along with the other things that come up in war times."

When community leaders arrived at the Grand Theater (once called the Grand Opera House) in the Labor Temple building for an announced patriotic meeting on the evening of April 11, five days after Congress had declared the United States at war, they found the waiting audience had already overflowed onto North Front Street, so they moved the meeting outdoors. Despite the coolness of the spring evening, the crowd followed banker John Hay, attorney W.A. Muir, hotel owner John Park, and the superintendent of schools, Mr. Munson, across the tracks, between trains, to the bandstand in the park on South Front Street, next to the depot. Neither the succession of six speakers nor the interruptions caused by passing trains discouraged the crowd that stayed to applaud stirring marches played by a band

Women at work as railroad section gang during World
War I. *Sweetwater County Historical Museum.*

and exhortations from the speakers, such as, "Rally to the
government in this grave crisis." "Keep the Kaiser from marching
into Paris." "It is a privilege to live in America."

One who undoubtedly would also have applauded and might
have been asked to speak, had he been there, was John Hay's
father-in-law, Archibald Blair, the town's most notable pioneer.
Blair for several years had been hobbling about with crutches. He
had stepped on a rusty nail and infection forced amputation of part
of one leg. During the long weeks of that miserably cold winter of
penetrating winds in 1917 he had been seriously ill. Two days
following the speech-making at the bandstand, Archie died; the
funeral was "the largest ever held in Rock Springs," according to
the *Rocket.*

The impact of the war was quickly evident in a number of ways. Men between twenty-one and thirty registered for military service; some in Rock Springs were summoned by their former homelands in Europe. Merchants curtailed free deliveries. A Liberty Day to rekindle patriotic support of the war brought more speeches during the afternoon, bonfires in the evening atop the hill back of No. 3 mine, and a minutes-long chorus from the mine whistles. The first shipment of knitted woolens—111 sweaters, 39 mufflers, and 31 pairs of socks—went off to the boys in training camps after they had been exhibited briefly in the window at Beeman and Neuber's store in the building on North Front that had once been "the company store."

First railroad officials and then government representatives, after the government took over the railroads in December 1917, expressed concern that the puffing of the busy locomotives might be halted by a shortage of fuel, despite record levels of coal production. Reflecting a widely held concern about the heavy consumption of alcohol throughout the nation, these officials blamed the threat of a coal shortage on some unpatriotic miners who, they said, spent more time in the saloons than they did in the mines. The Rock Springs city council ordered saloons closed between the hours of 10:00 P.M. and 7:00 A.M. but the early closing hour was largely ignored. The council later changed the closing hour to 11:00 P.M.

An evening of free entertainment, dancing, patriotic music, and, inevitably, speechmaking, sent off each contingent of "boys" headed for training camps. In Liberty Loan campaigns that sold government bonds Sweetwater County regularly exceeded its quotas. The head of these campaigns statewide was Mrs. T.S. Taliaferro of Rock Springs, long a leader in women's activities and in the Democratic party.

During the war self-appointed policemen of patriotism appeared across the United States in organizations such as the American Protective League, the American Defense Society, and a variety of "vigilance committees." Chapters of such groups were organized in at least eight Wyoming cities to watch aliens, spot sedition, and promote patriotism. One of these, a group called the

One Hundred Percent Club, appeared in Rock Springs for awhile, but its only publicly noted activity was furnishing speakers for send-off parties for draftees. Members of that group might have been involved in a more spontaneous type of instruction in patriotism when a man was beaten in Rock Springs because he "forgot he was not in Germany" by persons a newspaper identified only as "loyal citizens." He was also arrested and fined $59 in justice court on a charge not specified in the newspaper report. Another man who refused to buy war bonds was stripped, covered with yellow paint administered with a whisk broom, then coated with feathers and told to get out of town.

There were other examples of patriotic fervor breeding intolerance. High school classes in the German language were canceled and the teachers dismissed, Gisela (Bertagnolli) Wilde recalled, and the German textbooks burned. "Crystal" was substituted for "Vienna" in the name of a meat market and the Vienna Cafe became the Western Cafe. When the U.S. attorney general called for all Germans to register at the nearest police headquarters only twenty-one "German enemy aliens" responded in Rock Springs. Commented the editor of the *Rocket*: "We hope that is all there are among us. But it seems a small number."

As suddenly as it all began the war excitement ended. To celebrate the Armistice on Monday afternoon, November 11, 1918, Rock Springs residents took to the streets with whatever noise makers were handy. "Parades sprang up on a minute's notice," the *Rocket* reported, "some following a band and other crowds marching to the noise of tin pans and tubs. . . . The stores were closed . . . from Monday noon until after dark Tuesday." The celebration of the Armistice went on despite an anti-influenza quarantine that kept schools and theaters closed until November 15.

By the following March suppers and dances were being held at the Labor Temple for returning servicemen; most had been gone for less than a year. A few were returned much later—for funerals. That included the first Sweetwater County lad killed in the war, Thomas J. Whalen, and also Archibald L. Hay and Joseph Milbourne, who were killed in the greatest battle involving U.S.

troops, the bloody Argonne offensive that came shortly before the armistice. (The American Legion post in Rock Springs was named in honor of Archie Hay.)

By this time the excitement and the idealism of fighting a war to make the world safe for democracy were fading. The patriotic fervor of wartime was replaced by a suspicious intolerance on the part of some who were convinced radicals were behind every labor strike, every movement for change, every suggestion for reform. Suspicion became fear in the spring of 1919 when thirty-six bombs were found in packages mailed to prominent public officials and national business leaders. The U.S. attorney general's home in Washington, D.C., was bombed; there were riots in Cleveland; a bomb exploded on Wall Street.

The attorney general led a nationwide hunt for radicals, which was synonymous with reds, and he had a battalion of volunteer aides across the nation, including a new Ku Klux Klan, which had a "hate" list that included more than just "bolsheviks." Just being an alien was reason enough to be suspected, and few towns had a higher proportion of aliens than Rock Springs. Surprisingly, however, the "red scare" hysteria of 1919-1920 left no scars in Rock Springs. A cross was burned one night on the top of a ridge northwest of town, but that was all. No one in Rock Springs was arrested or deported as a dangerous alien. If the various patriotic groups were at work along Bitter Creek after the war, as they were many other places, they left no clear marks. There was, however, a bombing in Rock Springs in 1919, but it seems to have had no connection with the "red scare."

Back in 1913 John and Phillip Bertagnolli received a letter that threatened death if $2,000 was not left in a tin can at the No. 9 bridge. An attempt to trap the extortionist failed. John and Phillip were brothers who had come to Rock Springs from the Tyrol in the 1880s with their cousins, Henry and Leopoldo Bertagnolli. Henry tried working in the mines, while John and Phillip were street peddlers, selling shoestrings and nuts. Eventually the three men established the retail business that developed into the Union Mercantile and Supply Company. Leo was not one of the partners in that store, but he did, for a time, drive the store delivery wagon.

Archie Hay American Legion post monument in
Bunning Park, dedicated to Rock Springs men who
died in World War I. Originally the statue held a rifle
in its left hand. Somehow that hand and rifle were
broken off, leaving a wounded and perhaps more
poignant representation of the doughboy. *Photo by
Author.*

John, who never married, established branches of the store in Superior and Kemmerer, and became involved in other business ventures, including real estate. It was generally assumed that John was a wealthy man, especially after he built a large, two-story cement-block house, painted white with red trim, on J Street. The building was usually referred to in Rock Springs as "the villa." Phillip and his family lived there with John.

In 1917 John received another letter, bearing an impression of a black hand, demanding $10,000. "The Black Hand" or "Le Mano Nero" was the symbol of a criminal group in Sicily in the late nineteenth century. The black hand symbol was brought to the United States and used by various criminals and terrorists.

Again Bertagnolli ignored the demand for money, even though a short time later he found an unexploded bomb outside his house. Then, January 29, 1919, a few minutes after midnight an explosion shattered a large section of the front wall of the villa. Other homes in the area were also damaged by the force of the explosion. John was in Superior that night, but Phillip was sleeping in a front bedroom and he was injured in the explosion. His wife and small child in the back of the house were not hurt. No one was ever arrested for the crime; no further threats were received. Phillip and his family moved away from Rock Springs; John converted the villa into rented apartments, while he lived elsewhere until he died in 1936. The villa was demolished by a bulldozer in 1976 to make way for business buildings.

The bombing of the Bertagnolli house left most residents of Rock Springs stunned and frightened, but as months passed with no further violent incidents attention turned to other events, including the advent of Prohibition.

Frank Roncaglio operated a one-man early recycling
business in Rock Springs, collecting discarded items of
all kinds in this cart, which he pulled himself. A horse
would have to be fed and trucks he regarded as
unreliable. He was the father of Teno Roncalio, who
became a prominent attorney in Cheyenne and served
in Congress as Wyoming's representative. *Sweetwater
County Historical Museum.*

8

Moonshine, Flight, and Flood

Rock Springs achieved the status in 1900 of a "first class city." As spelled out in state law that meant a place with at least four thousand population. By any standard based on quality of life, the ex-coal camp only began to achieve some "class" in the 1920s. It was in that decade, when much of the nation seemed to be concentrating on the frivolous, that the town on Bitter Creek began to deal effectively with some of its worst problems, notably with the creek itself. In the early part of the decade, however, much attention was taken up with the new state and national laws banning alcoholic beverages and the effort, quite extensive in Rock Springs, to circumvent those laws. In addition, the town was intoxicated for a time by its involvement with the beginnings of the age of flight.

Monday evening, June 30, 1919, was a special night in Rock Springs, especially at the white house on the hill and at the Park Hotel, where dancing in the dining room and lobby continued until a "late hour." The next day, July 1, Wyoming went "dry," as had been decreed in a statewide referendum followed by legislative action, anticipating national Prohibition by six months. The OK Saloon on K Street opened as usual July 1—as a "coffee bar." Other saloon owners around town proclaimed their establishments converted to "soft drink parlors."

About a month later enforcement agents raided a vacant house on K Street where they dumped fifty-two gallons of whiskey. They also found a still at the end of a tunnel in the No. 4 district. That was the beginning of a decade-long but never successful effort to squelch the liquor trade in southwestern Wyoming. In addition to the Rock Springs area, the enforcement agents were especially active at Kemmerer and Diamondville, sixty miles northwest of Rock Springs. The highly prized Kemmerer moonshine was marketed by a well-organized underground system that reached as far as Chicago. Young Rock Springs men, often barely in their twenties, made top wages driving trucks laden with Kemmerer "moon" to Rock Springs, the central distribution point.

In the Rock Springs-Green River area during the Prohibition Era more than one hundred raids were made on private homes, soft drink parlors (the Rock Springs version of the speakeasy), and stills hidden in buildings or caves. The most extensive raid ever made by Prohibition enforcement agents in Wyoming swept through Sweetwater County in December 1921 when federal officers arrested sixty-two persons in Rock Springs, Green River, and Superior and confiscated 1,400 boxes of raisins, 3,000 gallons of "dago red" wine, and 1,000 gallons of other liquids judged to be illegally alcoholic. Fifteen bars (speakeasies) were searched and a number of private homes. Perhaps the largest moonshine still unearthed in Wyoming was in a cavern reported to be seventy feet long and forty feet wide in Cedar Mountain thirty-five miles south of Green River.

In a sweep in November 1923 of places suspected of selling home-made beer or wine with too much "kick," agents arrested eighteen persons and confiscated 345 bottles of beer and approximately 3,500 gallons of wine. That same year, in a raid on the white house on the hill, delicately described by the *Rocket* as "a questionable resort of this city," the agents uncovered only three gallons of moonshine but arrested two persons, including the madam, Cora Gray, and padlocked the place. The fancy house with its ornate bar and plush ballroom, scenes of gay revelry for at least two decades, fell into decay, occupied only by a caretaker. The police returned in 1925 to smash a moonshine still installed in the place, and shortly after that the place was demolished. That did not mean the end of prostitution in Rock Springs; it continued, primarily in second-floor rooms above K Street.

Wine making for consumption in the home was still permitted, and wine making had become an annual event in Rock

Springs after the southern Europeans began arriving. This activity reached its peak during the Prohibition years of the 1920s. As many as 100 carloads of grapes from California arrived in Rock Springs during September and October. The railroad would "spot" these loaded cars on the siding next to North Front Street where those who had ordered grapes came to claim their share, usually at least one-half ton and sometimes as much as two tons, at prices that varied over the years from $70 a ton to as much as $140. One customer every year was a 1913 immigrant from the village of Tuenno in the Tyrol's Val de Non, David Fedrizzi. David's wife had dutifully followed him to America in 1914, bringing with her their three small children and all the precious possessions she could cram into a large wooden trunk. David was a cooper and supported his family by fashioning wooden barrels ranging in size from five to fifty gallons, mostly used for holding wine. He also worked as a carpenter and laborer at the mines and rented out the grape press he had constructed for making wine. Each autumn, during the wine-making, that press was in use somewhere over a period of weeks as it was passed from house to house. It was estimated that enough wine, both red and white, was made each year in Rock Springs, Superior, and the other coal camps to supply each inhabitant with twenty gallons.

It was the best of times for Rock Springs, borne along with the nation on a general wave of prosperity, and also flushed by a lusty boom in coal mining in 1920. Coal miners were working forty hours a week, if they wanted to, at the highest wage ever: $7.92 an hour, gained in a November 1919 strike.

In the summer of 1920 excitement peaked along Bitter Creek when workmen began scraping the sagebrush off a flat area along Killpecker Creek north of town. Rock Springs, population 6,500 and still struggling to adapt to the automobile, was to have an airport, or at least a landing strip, one of fourteen sites across the continent where airmail planes would be landing.

The Post Office Department decided to try a transcontinental route after about two years of experience flying the mail between eastern cities. The aircraft used were war surplus De Havilland training planes with open cockpits and, some pilots said, "the gliding angle of a brick." The maximum altitude of these DH planes was 10,000 feet, a major factor in selection of a transcontinental route. This, and other considerations, made the Union Pacific route a logical choice; it never exceed 8,500 feet. Because the pilots could not navigate successfully at night, the mail service would have to be a combination of plane by day, train by night. In addition, the railroad tracks, the "iron compass" the pilots called them, would be a useful and comforting navigational aid during daylight hours. Landing strips were spaced along the railroad about every 300 miles, the range allowed by the fuel supply carried by the clumsy De Havillands. The Rock Springs field's nearest neighbors on the airmail route would be Cheyenne, 240 miles east, and Salt Lake City, 225 miles west.

The first airmail flight arrived from Cheyenne on a Wednesday morning in September 1920. The Rock Springs field was not a favorite of the pilots. They feared the soft runway and the strong and erratic winds that blasted down on the field from White Mountain on the west. During that first September of the airmail flights, three planes cracked up in Rock Springs. One ran off the landing strip and crashed into a ditch; a second one crashed immediately after takeoff; the pilot of the third could not find the landing strip so set his plane down on the flat just west of the old Chinatown area and coasted into the railroad tracks that led north to Reliance. None of the pilots were hurt.

The nation voted in November to put Warren G. Harding in the White House, the man who had said the country needed a return to "normalcy." By the time Harding was inaugurated in 1921 the coal boom had collapsed, and Rock Springs was in another "bust," which was normal in the sense of being a familiar pattern.

It seemed a poor time for a new theater to be opening. Construction of the Rialto had been started during the 1920 boom year with funds provided by local investors. After opening day in 1921 the Rialto's manager and part owner, Tom Berta, filled most of the twelve hundred seats most of the time with vigorous promotion. Admission to the movies was one dime for kids, and free for all on Labor Day and Eight-Hour Day (April 1), celebrating the anniversary of the establishment of the eight-hour shift in the mines. There was a free movie at Christmas time, too, paid for by the attorney, Douglas Preston, his treat for the kids. These free shows were the only ones some children saw during a year. On "Country Store" nights ticket buyers had a chance to win a bag of groceries. Berta stood on the stage to shout out the winning numbers in a great booming voice that matched his stature. Most theaters of the time had piano players to accompany the silent movies with music attuned to the dramatic action on the screen, but the Rialto had a six-piece orchestra (later enlarged to ten) directed by John J. Brueggemann.

Every Sunday the movies were replaced by vaudeville acts brought from Salt Lake, and sometimes Berta booked touring troupes traveling via the railroad, including the Metropolitan Opera Singers. The Rialto also served as the principal theater for local-talent performances, which the community supported enthusiastically. One of Berta's favorite performers was Art Rosatti, son of Tyrolean immigrants, printer for income, accordian player for fun. Berta also invited the glee clubs from various schools to perform at the theater during intermissions of regularly scheduled shows. Berta's Rialto Amusement Company, later acquired the Grand Theater where he also showed movies and staged boxing and wrestling matches.

Tom Berta was the town's leading bon vivant. He was a large, lusty, and generous extrovert with a lively sense of humor. Seldom was he without a cigar as he served as master of ceremonies for community meetings, busily arranged local talent musical programs, directed community fund drives, or hosted parties in his apartment above the Rialto, where the refreshments were always plentiful although, in the Prohibition Era, illegal.

The principal competition to his theater during the twenties came from the Rex, which was the battered and seedy old Oracle made resplendent in new dress: cushioned chairs, draperies, fresco decorations, mirrored foyer, and new electrified marquee. The manager and man behind the rebirth of this theater was James Sartoris, orchestra and band leader and music teacher, the principal competitor to Brueggemann, director of music at the

Two De Havilland planes and the hangar at the Rock
Spring airmail field in 1920. *Sweetwater County Historical
Museum.*

Rialto. By 1924 the enterprising Berta and his Rialto Amusement
Company owned all three theaters in town, including the Rex.

The Union Pacific Coal Company decided to move most of its
executive offices to Rock Springs from Omaha and Cheyenne
(except the president's office in Omaha), constructing a circle of
homes on the south edge of town for housing its executives and
their families. The area was named Wardell Court; it remains
today but the houses are now privately owned. The clubhouse,
which the company also built there, was often used for community
events until it became a residence for student nurses in training at
the hospital.

Late in 1921, Rock Springs residents watched, perhaps with
visions of another Salt Creek oil boom dancing in their heads, as
carloads of material for drilling rigs and well casings were
unloaded and trucked south to the Quaking Asp Mountain area in
Baxter Basin. Only three years earlier the great oil gushers in
central Wyoming's fabulous Salt Creek field had boosted the
population of 2,000 in the town of Casper by tenfold in a few
months.

At the airfield there were moments of excitement as well. A favorite excursion for those who had autos was to drive the few miles north to the airfield to watch the airmail planes come and depart; sometimes there were crackups. The pilot who had the most problems with the Rock Springs field was H.C. Collison. In 1921 a sudden gust of wind flipped his plane as he was taking off; he was not hurt. Later the same year he had engine trouble over Point of Rocks but landed safely on the gravel surface of the Lincoln Highway. About three months later he cracked up on another takeoff but survived again. Another pilot, Walter Bunting, was not so lucky. His De Havilland plunged to the ground and exploded into flames shortly after takeoff from the Rock Springs strip. Bunting was the first fatality at the Rock Springs field, one of eighteen who died in the first three years of the transcontinental airmail service.

Pilot Bob Ellis, who was credited with shooting down four German planes during World War I, survived to tell about the most unusual accident at the Rock Springs field. It happened in January 1922.

> I took off with the regular westbound mail in a strong head wind, circled the field, attaining an altitude of 9,200 feet, about 2000 feet above the hills, and headed for Salt Lake. While attempting to cross the hill [White Mountain] just west of the field, the ship was caught in a terrific down draft, which despite the fact that I had on a full motor, carried me down with great speed into the side of the mountain. Just before hitting the ground, I cut the switches, and pulled the stick all the way back. After striking the ground the plane slid backward about fifty feet and stopped at an angle of at least eighty degrees, the side of the mountain being almost perpendicular.
>
> I rolled the sacks of mail about 1,500 feet to the bottom of the canyon to be taken back to the field.

Mechanics later climbed up to dismantle the plane, removed it in pieces to the airfield below, reassembled it, and got it flying again.

The De Havillands could fly no faster than 110 miles an hour, but one pilot covered the 240 miles between Rock Springs and Cheyenne in one hour and thirty-two minutes, a speed of about 160 miles an hour. Going the other direction another plane the same day made an average speed of about 40 miles an hour. A wind, estimated at 60 miles an hour, made the difference.

By the early months of 1922 the mines were working only part-time and housewives were shopping frugally. In April they were pinching every penny as the miners started a strike that lasted until August when they won an agreement to keep the pay rate set in 1920. That rate remained in force until 1924.

Because of a coal industry gone stagnant, the economy in Rock Springs was listless while most of the nation concentrated on a spree of making and spending money. But there were moments of good cheer in 1922. A drilling rig hit it big in Baxter Basin in August—not oil, but gas, the beginning of a new major industry for the area. In October the Rock Springs high school football team won the first game it ever played, defeating Evanston 19-0. In fact, the Miners, later renamed Tigers, were the best on the rocky gridirons in southwestern Wyoming that year; they won the only two football games played in the area, both with Evanston.

The man who might well have won a contest for the title of first citizen of Rock Springs, John Hay, was thought to be a shoo-in as Republican candidate for governor in the general election in 1922, but he bore some baneful burdens. One was the animosity carried over from a fierce primary campaign. In addition he was viewed by many as the candidate of the Union Pacific and the coal industry and by the "drys" as the candidate of the "wettest town" in a legally dry state. Hay lost to the Democrat, William B. Ross, Cheyenne lawyer, by 723 votes.

March 1, 1923, Eugene McAuliffe became president of the Union Pacific Coal Company. He was the son of a staff officer in the British army who moved his family to the Dakota Territory in the United States in 1873. McAuliffe learned railroading and eventually joined the Union Pacific. Soon after he was appointed head of the coal company he initiated a safety program designed to reduce accidents in the mines. It was several years before the miners, who had a stubbornly fatalistic attitude about mine accidents, began to respond. But McAuliffe made workers in mines with the best safety records eligible for prize drawings, in which the top prize was a new automobile, won the support of the elderly miners by organizing a club and celebration to recognize the "old timers," and established an annual field day when miners and Boy Scouts competed in first aid contests. He eventually made the U.P. mines national leaders in safety.

Beginning in June 1925 when 283 employees who had been with the company at least twenty years joined the Old Timers Association, Old Timers' Day became one of the major holidays in Rock Springs, involving miners from all the U.P. mines in the Rock Springs district and Hanna. Nearly always McAuliffe was one of the speakers, and the day after was set aside for the annual first aid contests when teams from the various coal camps competed in providing first aid for "victims" of simulated accidents. For both adults and youngsters who participated, it was one of the major events of each year.

The events that marked every holiday along Bitter Creek were a mixture of favorite American and European activities. There were nearly always speeches, parades, local talent entertainment, free movies for children, musical programs, sports such as baseball and other games (including quoits, bocci bolli, and pie throwing contests), nail driving for women, and often a banquet. The southern European's love for festivals and fun tended to be dominant in Rock Springs, not the austere traditions of the New England Yankee, and the activities also had the lusty flavor of the frontier.

The biggest celebrations in Rock Springs took place the first week in April for Eight-Hour Day, and the first week in September for Labor Day; celebrating for both usually extended over more than one day. In the twenties most Rock Springs miners remembered the 1890s when the United Mine Workers of America organized and won the battle for an eight-hour day in the mines, a recognition, as the Eight-Hour Day speakers sometimes phrased it, of the "miner's right to live."

For approximately twenty years every parade was led by a

drum major, A.G. Griffiths, who was once a member of the British Grenadier Guards and a veteran of military service in the Egyptian Sudan and the South African Boer War. He arrived in Rock Springs in 1905, worked in the mines, and appeared each holiday resplendent in a uniform bedecked with braid, buttons, and medals until his death in 1926.

For four years, beginning in 1924 and lasting until 1928, a period when the new Ku Klux Klan was preaching its restricted view of white, Protestant Americanism in many parts of the United States, Rock Springs proudly staged an annual tribute to ethnic diversity. This was International Night, which despite its short life, is often cited as one of the major triumphs in the history of Rock Springs. It began when the Reverend Stephen Pyle of the First Baptist Church, in his role as good fellowship chairman of the Lions Club, brought to a club meeting a number of guests with musical talents and representing various nationalities. The club members were so intrigued they decided to sponsor an expanded evening program at the Elks Club, featuring the variety of backgrounds in the town's population. Many played roles in developing this popular show, including the Reverend J.V. Tkoch who had only arrived in Rock Springs in 1924 to serve as the priest for the Eastern Christian Orthodox Church in western Wyoming. His flock included Greek, Slavic, Bulgarian, Rumanian, and Dalmation immigrants. Tkoch and later the Reverend Thorotheas Pappas of the Greek Orthodox Church were major influences in helping to perserve the traditions of Greek culture in the life of Rock Springs.

Eventually the International Night show was moved to the Rialto Theater, to accommodate more of the throng that came to see it. Two shows were presented in 1928, one in January, when two thousand crammed into the Rialto and another two thousand were turned away, and another in December, when the show was given twice in one night to a packed house. The program varied from year to year, but the performers in the final program were Scots, Slovaks, Tyroleans, Croatians, Japanese, Italians, and Slovenes. The program opened with the stage filled with costumed persons carrying candles. As a man from Scotland used the flame of his candle to light the one held by a woman from Switzerland standing next to him he said in English, "As light begets light, so love begets love the world around." Thus the flame was passed through the line of fifty-one persons, and each repeated the sentence, but in fifty other languages, including languages of three American Indian tribes. Lavish exhibits prepared by various groups were displayed at the Elks Club.

Bands and music of all sorts were an integral part of Rock Springs celebrations, to a considerable extent due to the influence of local music teachers, particularly James Sartoris and John Brueggemann. State high school competitions, usually held in Laramie in the spring, included more than a basketball tourney in the twenties. In 1923 Leno Ceretto of Rock Springs, a student of Brueggemann, won first place in violin playing. That was the first of seven successive state championships won by Brueggemann's students. In 1924 when basketball teams entered in the state tourney at Laramie were classified according to average weight, Rock Springs won eight games in five days to claim the state championship. At the same time, another Brueggemann student, Sylvan Ward, repeated as violin champion, and Clara Boyle took the first-place trophy for excellence in shorthand. When the triumphant youngsters arrived back in Rock Springs on a Sunday evening train, a cheering throng was waiting at the depot. An impromptu parade led by a band marched through a downtown area aglow with red torches, ending at the Elks Club for a reception.

It was an era of heightened interest in sports, partly generated by the ballyhoo gleefully published by most of the big city newspapers. It was the era of Bobby Jones in golf, Babe Ruth in baseball, Bill Tilden in tennis, the Jack Dempsey-Gene Tunney contests in the boxing ring, and the "galloping ghost of Illinois," the great Red Grange, one of the heroes of the college gridirons. So, Rock Springs in toasting its local sports heroes and developing its own sporting activities was only following a national trend. School sports were popular for another reason in Rock Springs, as Tom Manatos recalled, "For some making a high school team was the only way to get to go on trips out of town."

People in other towns thought Rock Springs' athletic success was based on "big tough miners." "It wasn't that our players were so big," Tom said, "they were just competitive."

During 1923, the year Bobby Jones first won the National Open in golf, the affluent of Rock Springs decided it was time to bring the brassie and the niblick to Rock Springs. To that end a few men drove ten miles south of town to Kent's Ranch which, they agreed, was a beautiful setting for a golf course. Despite the fact the ground was still covered by snow, they laid out a course. Later when the snow melted they learned every fairway was liberally strewn with rocks. Undaunted, they established a nine-hole course with sand greens and a clubhouse. Antelope, frequently, and deer, occasionally, halted their own "play on the range" to watch as golfers chased errant balls that careened off boulders into a "rough" that deserved the name.

The owner of the ranch, William Kent, who was born in England, came to Rock Springs in the 1880s, worked for the U.P. Coal Company for awhile, and then bought this land north of Quaking Asp Mountain. It included a pleasant, green oasis along a creek that ran near the ranch house, and Kent made it available for outdoor recreation, a favorite picnic spot for Rock Springs residents. About two years after the golf club at Kent's Ranch was started another group of forty cleared away enough brush and rock for nine golf holes on the south edge of town. They laid cocoa mats for tees and oiled sand for greens, and called their layout the Dead Horse Canyon Gulf Club, because the area involved had been a dumping ground for the carcasses of dead horses. A good drive on this course could also be turned into disaster when the ball struck a rock as it landed. Frequently it then careened off into the sagebrush rough or into a ten-foot deep gulley, probably never to be found. When the two clubs merged in 1927 only the Dead Horse Canyon links survived. Some members thought Dead Horse Canyon an inappropriate name, so it was changed to the Boulder Golf and Country Club. But then a visitor played the course one day, and later word reached Rock Springs that friends at his hometown in the East were enthralled with his tale of the Dead Horse Canyon links. The club reinstated that name and adopted a symbol of a coiled rattlesnake acting as a tee for a golf ball. Players said they regularly carried "snake irons" in their golf bags.

In the mid-twenties the critical issue in Rock Springs was still the railroad crossing at C Street where traffic was increasing because the Lincoln Highway had been routed through Rock Springs by way of the crossing. Although railroad traffic was not as heavy as it had been during the war years, there was still enough to block the crossing about once each hour. In addition, the nerves of residents were on edge much of the time because of the shrill cacophonous whistling of the locomotives as engineers communicated with train crews. One short, apply brakes; two long, release brakes; one long three short, flagman protect rear of train, and so on through day and night. The situation was described as an "intolerable nuisance" and "a blight on growth and progress." The blocked crossing could be more than a nuisance. It was the only direct way to get an injured person from the north side to the hospital on the south, and the only way the fire department at city hall could send men and equipment north. The consequences were illustrated when a U.P. warehouse burned down one day while the firemen were delayed at the crossing.

The railroad was not adamantly uncooperative. In an effort to provide relief, it ordered switching on the tracks between North and South Front streets halted during peak periods of crossing traffic; trains were cut to clear the crossing when a lengthy stop was expected; eastbound freight trains were parked at the Blairtown sidings while their locomotives puffed alone to coal and water replenishment stations at the center of town, and the company was considering plans for moving the switching yards.

A city election campaign was nearing its climax, at the time, with the leading contractor in the town, P.C. Bunning, as the Democratic candidate for mayor, opposing the incumbent Republican, Harry G. Parker. Bunning's campaign advertising proclaimed that he would "stand for advancement of Rock Springs," but neither candidate made a specific promise to end the crossing crisis, which could only be ended with the cooperation of the Union Pacific.

Buildings along Bitter Creek in central section of Rock Springs with coal chutes on mainline U.P. tracks in background. This section of the creek was filled in and it became part of Noble Drive street after the 1924 flood. *Sweetwater County Historical Museum.*

Flood on Bitter Creek. Date of this photo is not known, but it may have been taken during the 1924 flood. *Sweetwater County Historical Museum.*

Peter Christian Bunning, a native of Germany where he had learned coopering (wooden barrel making), was sixty-five years old when he took over the mayor's office at the city hall he had helped build as a common laborer. Bunning also had helped lay some of the extra tracks along North Front Street when he was employed as a railroad section hand after he arrived in Rock Springs in 1886. After a brief stint as the town's night marshal, he started an express and draying business, which he turned over to his son in 1917 when he became a contractor in road construction and other earth-moving work. Bunning's firm was the major contractor in construction of the first highway between Rock Springs and Green River and in digging the drainage ditch intended to control the water from cloudbursts south of town.

Bunning took office in January; in March he was hospitalized with injuries from an auto accident. In April the town was hit by possibly the most devastating flood of its history. An unusually warm early spring melted a heavy layer of snow on the hills to the east and south of Rock Springs. As the brown, murky water in the creek rose rapidly Friday night, April 4, residents of the dugouts in the eastern section of town began packing belongings and heaving furniture up on the creek bank above their shacks. The flood rose steadily during the weekend and finally reached a peak depth of fifteen feet in some places on Tuesday. The dugouts filled with water and some were swept away. The flooding was clearly aggravated by obstructions created by the dugouts, outhouses, animal pens, and other structures in the channel the creek had carved for itself with floods of previous years. No persons lost their lives in 1924, but many were left homeless; all children reported missing turned up unharmed; losses in rabbits, pigs, and chickens were heavy. An electric washing machine, wine barrels, and a large whiskey still were among items spotted floating westward with the torrent.

That admired early citizen of Rock Springs, David G. Thomas, the beloved "Davy Tom" to the Chinese, mayor in 1900 and 1901, judge, and unofficial poet laureate, one time penned a piece about Bitter Creek in which he wrote:

O, Classic Creek! rich in tradition
Of tragedy and superstition;
Your yearly, reckless inundation
Provides the means of sanitation;
Besides, the Lord knows very well
When you have purged yourself of smell
And other things that much displease
You've freed the town of foul disease.

Immediately after the injured Mayor Bunning returned to duty he initiated discussion with the city council about flood control and a sanitary sewer but then delayed further planning until the Union Pacific's views could be heard. The U.P. officials suggested the creek could be diverted away from North Front Street and the central part of town. The plan would eliminate a section of the creek that flowed south, approximately parallel to and east of M Street, until it made a sharp, elbowlike turn just below the railroad tracks to flow back to the northwest and its junction with Killpecker Creek.

A plan of four parts was settled upon:

Follow the U.P. plan to rechannel Bitter Creek into a course north of the central part of town, a course the creek had once used many years before, and make it adequate to handle future floods.

Provide land for new housing away from the creek for those who had been living in the creek dugouts.

Fill in the old channel that slashed that broad V-shaped gully through the section of town north of the tracks.

Construct a sanitary sewer system now, not just for the south section, but for all of what was reported to be the largest town in the United States without a sewer system.

Strong support for the plan came from many, including Dr. Oliver Chambers, U.P. Coal Company doctor, who had for years feared the threat of the open sewer so aptly called Bitter Creek. Another was Father Anton Schiffrer, who recognized its promise for the members of his North Side Catholic Church congregation, mostly Slavic Catholics he had been struggling to help since he first came to Rock Springs in 1910. He had celebrated his first mass at the North Side church on Christmas Eve 1912, when the church was nothing more than a basement. The congregation continued to meet in the basement for years while painstakingly accumulating funds to finish the church a bit at a time.

The voters would be asked to approve a double bond issue to build the sanitary system and creek diversion for flood control. But would the Union Pacific support a bond issue? The answer came quickly. Said a letter over the signature of the coal company president, Eugene McAullife, "While we are the heaviest taxpayers in the city, we are willing to go along . . . in all reasonable plans for improvement." The railroad not only went along; it donated land for the diversion channel. It also released other land for sale to the "squatters" who were being pushed out of the creek bed. A bond issue of $425,000 for the sewer was approved, and when the time came for the bonds to be sold John Hay announced that his Rock Springs National Bank would buy the entire issue.

With dragline and horse-drawn scoops 75,000 cubic feet of sand and rocks were dug out to form the new creek channel and used to fill in the old channel; when filled it was paved over to form new streets; one of them was named Channel Street.

While the creek rechanneling and sewer construction projects were underway the town's two Catholic churches were busy with their own improvement projects. Pleased to see arrangements being made to get the residents in the dugouts out of the creek bed and into decent housing, Father Schiffrer turned his efforts to completing his north side Catholic church building. This was finally accomplished in December 1925, thirteen years after he held the first services in the basement. For many in Rock Springs it is still the North Side Catholic Church, but it was formally named the Church of Saints Cyril and Methodius, for the Greek brothers who were known as the "Apostles to the Slavs" after they were sent by the pope in Rome as missionaries to Moravia (today's central Czechoslovakia). Father Schiffrer was also holding services in Superior, which he reached by horseback usually,

Photo above shows a part of the Bitter Creek channel as it was in 1920, which after 1924 was incorporated into Bunning Park, shown below. *Top photo from the Sweetwater County Historical Museum. Bottom photo by the Author.*

although sometimes he made the twenty-mile trip on foot, until his faltering health forced him to leave the high altitude of the Rock Springs area.

Father Schiffrer's work on the north side was matched on the south side by Father S.A. Welsh, who arrived in Rock Springs in 1918. Father Welsh was born in New Jersey, educated at eastern colleges, and came to Rock Springs one month after his ordination at St. Patrick's Cathedral in New York City. He found a neglected parish where only two families regularly attended services, and he faced boorish taunting and even physical abuse on the streets of Rock Springs from bullies who scorned his eastern manners. He stopped the abuse because he was courageous, physically large and strong, and a trained boxer. He revived the parish through long hours of hard work and got Our Lady of Sorrows Church built by 1926.

Nor was Chris Bunning through with his improvement projects. He was reelected mayor four times, and during his succession of two-year terms he pushed through a $295,000 street-paving program, created a five-acre city park on land reclaimed by the creek diversion project and donated to the city by the Union Pacific, and improved the street-lighting system and the storm water draining canals.

A revealing word picture of mayor and city council debating issues midst clouds of smoke came from the typewriter of Louis C. Phillips, news editor of the *Rocket* for a brief period and one of the most competent in the century-long parade of journalists through Rock Springs. Phillips wrote:

> There's Mayor Chris Bunning, sitting at the end of the table where he can get a good view of all his cabinet. His ever-present cigar shoved deep in his cheek, he gruffly prods the evening's business to completion. Watch him work and you know who's running Rock Springs.
>
> An individualist is Councilman Angus Hatt. He's the "left winger" of the council, almost always the only member of the group who will risk opposing suggestions of the mayor and who will battle verbally with him.

Rock Springs' "Silent Cal" is Councilman Frank Holmes. He listens intently to what goes on in the discussions—but when he makes a comment, that's news. He has been known to attend a meeting without saying more than two words. Those two are "present" and "aye." He says the first when the roll is called. The second he says when the vote on a motion for adjournment is taken.

Always in attendance, too, was editor Frank Crumley of the *Miner*, incessantly smoking cigarettes despite the fact he supplied the council with a dozen good cigars every meeting night, and Fire Chief Forndran, who insisted his pipe did not smell, and, back in a corner, likeable Jim Harris, the chief of police.

Before the decade of the twenties ended the U.P. Coal Company also contributed an improvement that greatly pleased the miners' wives, at least. That was a bathhouse where miners could shower immediately after coming off shift. Rock Springs households were at last freed of the tyranny of the grimy coal dust carried home on clothes and body by the weary miners. The ritual of the tub of hot water by the kitchen stove was happily abolished, and this delighted the miners' children as much as anyone, because theirs was the chore of emptying the bath water outside the back door. That in turn meant the end of the ice pond that covered much of the backyard most of the winter. Miners' families were also allowed to use the bathhouse at special times during the week. But the bathhouse showers did not wash away the "miners' tattoo," blue lines and spots on their hands. It was caused by coal dust that penetrated scratches and cuts; healing covered the dust but it was still visible under the new skin as blue markings.

During the twenties, Rock Springs was far from the sporting big city centers of "the jazz age," but it had movies, the most popular form of entertainment of the era and from which the rising generation was getting many of its ideas; it also had the automobile, which gave the new generation new freedom; and radios, which provided another new form of entertainment as well as education and information. Radio and movies speeded up the trend for Rock Springs to become more like the rest of the United

Looking west from the top of the pedestrian overpass.
Photo taken in 1920s. *Sweetwater County Historical
Museum.*

States. Before the end of the decade you could go to the Rialto for one of the new "talkies," or you could go join the fun at the new dance hall, the Playmore, built in 1928. Admission was one dollar for gents, only ten cents for ladies, and generally the two came separately; escorting a date to the Playmore was uncommon. At the Playmore most dancers learned the Charleston and a few the tango, but neither displaced the perennial favorite in Rock Springs, the polka. Imported from its native land of Bohemia in 1884, the polka had been named in honor of the Poles, heroes of a peasant uprising in eastern Europe. No evening in a Rock Springs dance hall could be declared complete without at least one playing of the rollicking "Beer Barrel Polka."

Saturday nights on the way to the dance hall, you could stop at any one of a number of places for a glass of Dago red wine or a shot of "Kemmerer moon," even fill a flask to take along. Anti-liquor raids had virtually ceased in the Rock Springs area by 1929.

9

The Turbulent Thirties

In contrast to the heady prosperity that seemed to pervade much of the nation, the Rock Springs economy was sluggish again in 1928 because of a depressed market for coal. A new agreement had dropped the miners' pay by more than one dollar to $6.72 for an eight-hour day. Some miners also grumbled about the increased mechanization of the mines. McAuliffe argued that miners who learned to use the digging and loading machines would be making more than ever, because the pay rate for machine operators was about two dollars higher than the base rate.

Despite the slowdown at the coal mines, bank deposits were up. Early in 1928 Claude Elias, cashier of the Rock Springs National Bank, told the Lions Club members that their city was a wealthy one, compared with others in Wyoming. Bank deposits, he said, had more than doubled in ten years to a total that would, if divided evenly, give nearly one thousand dollars to each resident, the highest per capita figure among Wyoming cities.

Other good news came in March: the basketball team won the state championship again. That turned out to be what might be called the inaugural of a golden age of high school athletics in Rock Springs. When school opened in September 1929 candidates for the football team reported for the first practice wondering about the new coach, who had come down from a little burg called Cokeville up to the northwest in the Star Valley area of Wyoming. His name was Claire Blanchard, but everybody soon learned to call him Okie. Under his guidance the Rock Springs High School teams reigned as athletic lords of the southwestern Wyoming district for the next eight years.

During 1927 the U.P. Coal Company had opened its new store and office building, and it also added the sound of bagpipes, played by McAuliffe's Kiltie Band, to the Rock Springs holiday celebrations that year and thereafter. This was not the first time the skirling of bagpipes had been heard on the banks of the Bitter Creek because when Murray Noble of Edinburgh, Scotland, came to Rock Springs in 1891 he brought a set of pipes, which he often played on Sunday mornings. McAuliffe's Kiltie Band was organized and outfitted by the coal company in the uniform of the Forty-second Royal Highlanders, the "Black Watch," and the tartan of the Stuarts at a cost of $10,000. In the beginning the members were all Scotsmen, but replacements in later years added at least a half dozen other nationalities.

In the fall of 1928, about the time the fabulous bull market hit its peak on an ecstatic Wall Street in New York City, the paving, curbs, and gutters of the Rock Springs street improvement project were being completed. City officials were threatening to send employees around to padlock outdoor toilets still in use if owners did not hook up to the sanitary sewer. The city and the U.P. railroad were sparring again about the possibility of an underpass to replace the C Street crossing, an increasing frustration in a town now at 8,500 in population. Growth troubled the phone company as well with a directory of nearly 1,500 numbers and some users still wanting to rely on the memories of the switchboard operators. One phone company employee, the bookkeeper and former operator, Jennie Fortuna, did know more than half of them.

Hopes for a major oil field discovery in the Rock Springs area kept rebounding from successive disappointments. A near parade of geologists, potential investors, and oil-drilling experts came to survey the Baxter Basin area during the twenties, each visit accompanied by speculation about an "impending boom." What the drillers discovered mostly were great underground pockets of natural gas, which could only be valuable if somehow gotten to urban areas where it could be used as fuel. Early one morning in November 1928 a new big gasser on the south slope of Quaking Asp Mountain came in with a roar heard in Rock Springs, ten miles away. Convinced that this and a half dozen other wells justified the effort, three firms formed a holding company to build a pipeline. Beginning in January 1929, in one of the most severe winters ever recorded in southwestern Wyoming, construction crews laid 300 miles of pipeline from the Baxter Basin, south and east of Rock Springs, over mountains, under rivers, across sagebrush desert to the cities of Utah finishing the job in August. "Pipeline 29" cost $24 million. Out of the pipeline project came the Mountain Fuel Supply Company, which became a major employer in the Rock Springs area. The coming of natural gas was not an unmixed blessing for Rock Springs. It was clean, convenient, and when the time came when it was cheaper than coal, gas quickly cut into the market for coal.

In October 1929, shortly after President Herbert Hoover had announced that the United States was near "the final triumph over poverty," came the stupifying crash on Wall Street. In a matter of months millions of investors had lost their savings. Businesses closed their doors; factory assembly lines ground to a halt; bank doors were locked. Millions found themselves walking the streets searching for jobs. The Great Depression had begun. Early in 1930, however, a *Rocket* headline proclaimed "Prosperity on Wing" along Bitter Creek, which was a bit ambiguous since it could mean flying away. But the text clearly indicated its intended meaning was flying high. U.P. Coal Company President McAuliffe agreed, predicting a "good year." The U.P. mines were back to working six days a week, and many large bands of sheep were wintering on surrounding desert lands, suggesting that the spring lamb and wool crop would bring thousands of dollars to the area.

So the crash of the stock market created far less of a shock wave in Rock Springs than what happened on Sunday, May 18, 1930, when thirteen Rock Springs city officials, one county officer, and thirty-eight others were arrested on indictments from a federal grand jury charging conspiracy to violate the Prohibition laws. Federal agents had apparently abandoned the periodic raids, which had failed to check the extensive liquor trade in Rock Springs, and turned to gathering evidence for the conspiracy charges. The men arrested included Mayor Bunning; three

Above: Street dance on Broadway (Fourth Street) probably in the 1930s. **Below:** South Front Street in the 1940s. Commercial Hotel at right. *Both, Sweetwater County Historical Museum.*

councilmen, Matt Steffenson, Charles Gregory, and Frank Holmes: former Councilman John Dykes; City Attorney Fred W. Johnson; Chief of Police James Harris; Police Judge Ed Johnson; City Treasurer Ralph Harns; Deputy Sheriff George Harris; and four city policemen, John Veronda, Joe Davenport, Sam Ryder, and Val Marcina. The only city patrolman to escape indictment, William Harvey, was named acting police chief over a staff of five quickly sworn in as "acting policemen." The federal charge was that the defendants had conspired to violate the Prohibition Act with a licensing system and frequent "fines." The charge against the city officials of licensing illegal liquor outlets was based on the Rock Springs taxation system, which had been established back in the nineteenth century, a system based on occupation taxes levied against each business in town. The other thirty-eight defendants who were not public officials were accused of selling liquor under occupation tax "licenses." Many were proprietors of "soft drink parlors," which with good reason the federal investigator in the case suggested were unusually numerous in Rock Springs. Trial was held before a jury in the federal court in Cheyenne July 2; all were acquitted.

That was in essence the last roundup for the antiliquor forces in Rock Springs. Three years later there was a scramble to get licenses to sell beer, by then legalized by new action of the state legislature. Six railway carloads of beer arrived and were spotted, still locked, near the freight depot until one minute after midnight May 13, 1933. Then the cars were opened and the beer transferred to waiting trucks, which sped off to crowded restaurants and soft drink parlors that had retail licenses from the city council. Thus was the beginning of the end of Prohibition celebrated in Rock Springs. But since this was 3.2 beer, speakeasies, where one could get a drink with much higher alcohol content, remained popular. When the prohibition against the "hard stuff" was finally lifted in 1935 and sale of liquor placed under the strict control of a state licensing authority, Rock Springs was told its quota of saloons was eighteen, less than half the number that existed before Prohibition. An appeal by the city council on behalf of the anguished former saloon keepers got that increased to twenty-five. The two largest Wyoming cities, Cheyenne and Casper, each had only twenty retail liquor licenses.

Before the saloons returned, the wings of prosperity in Rock Springs had been severely clipped. Although the sheep business continued to grow, with more than 250,000 head on winter ranges in 1932, the coal business had collapsed again. Miners worked an average of only 155 days in 1931; coal production was down in the Rock Springs area by 21 percent. Some commercial mines had been abandoned. The United Mine Workers, shaken by internal revolt that erupted into warfare with brass knuckles, blackjacks, pick handles, and even guns in the Midwest, had to accept another wage cut, down to $5.42 a day, the lowest in thirteen years, but "the best possible under distressed economic conditions," the mine owners said. The railroad, facing increased truck and bus competition, took ten trains off the tracks in 1932; that eliminated the annual need for 43,000 tons of coal, a month and a half of work in a single mine. The coal business was also feeling the effects of competition with natural gas. Businessmen and both railroad and mine union officials joined to organize a "Ship by Rail, Burn Coal Committee" in an effort to win customers for the basic industries in the town.

Hoboes, waiting to catch trains east or west, camped out in areas along the creek west of town, some building shelters of scrap wood and cardboard. The town set up a soup kitchen, which in its first 114 days served 4,012 meals at a cost of eleven cents a meal; the VFW conducted food drives for the needy; the city organized a Mayor's Relief Committee to help an estimated 250 families without money, food, or clothing. Salvation Army meals, served both local indigents and transients, included mush and toast for breakfast and meat stew for lunch.

By 1932 all the veteran Chinese miners had either died or returned to their homeland. Nine were given pensions and sent back to China in 1925 after a banquet in their honor at the Grand Cafe, operated then and since by Chinese. The oldest of the nine was seventy-six; the average age of the group was sixty-nine; their average years of employment in the U.P. mines was thirty-three. In the following two years eight more were similarly feted and sent "home" to finish their lives in comparative luxury. Lao Che (Jim, the stable boss) returned to Canton in 1929 and the final contingent of three left in 1932.

In March 1932 the high school basketball team played in the state tournament at Casper. In the semifinals, the Tigers survived a game with Lyman in which the score was 2 to 2 at the end of the first quarter, and 16 to 16 at the end of four quarters. Rock Springs won in the overtime period by a score of 17 to 16. In the title game that followed, Rock Springs defeated Cheyenne 18 to 11. When high school enrollment more than tripled during the twenties, the school district erected a new building at the foot of No. 1 hill. There a grateful Karl Winchell, principal, and his faculty enrolled more than seven hundred in the fall of 1932. There was enough space to put eighty first and second graders in the building as well. A stadium next to the new high school was finished in 1934, with the help of federal relief funds, on ground formerly occupied by a small mountain of slack and cinders from the No. 1 mine; the wall around the stadium was constructed of stones saved when the old rock school on B Street was torn down.

In the thirties a new section of the Lincoln Highway was finished that entered and left Rock Springs on the north side of town, avoiding the infamous C Street crossing, but funds were needed to finish the connecting link through Rock Springs. Funds came from the federal programs designed to provide work for the unemployed, and the U.P. railroad donated land for new right-of-way sections. Federal funding also helped with improvements at the airport, painting the city hall, widening storm ditches, and shoring up the banks of Bitter Creek.

In the Democratic primary election of 1933 an auto salesman named E.A. Chester defeated Chris Bunning in his bid for a sixth term as mayor, then Chester was defeated in the general election by a lawyer, Republican Walter Muir.

In the spring of 1934, not long after Bunning observed his seventy-fifth birthday, one hundred business and professional men of Rock Springs gathered at the Elks Home for a turkey dinner prepared and served by the ladies of the Episcopal Guild. The dinner was followed by a program honoring Peter Christian

Above: The sign spanning C Street was erected about 1930 with one-half the funds supplied by coal mine owners and the other half raised by a popular subscription drive organized by the Lions Club. It was recycled into a sign for the Western Wyoming Community College about 1980 and now stands on College Hill. **Below:** The Kiltie Band was organized in 1927, shown here in their Stuart tartan and the uniform of the Forty-second Royal Highlanders, the "Black Watch." Sponsorship of the band was assumed by the Rock Springs Chamber of Commerce after the U.P. Coal Company was dissolved. *Both, Sweetwater County Historical Museum.*

Bunning, who was presented with a solid gold twenty-one-jewel Hamilton hunting case watch. There were speeches, of course, and the principal one was delivered by Eugene McAuliffe, the man who had suggested the testimonial dinner. The music for the evening, appropriate for a man born in Germany, was furnished by a German band under the direction of Jim Sartoris. Sixteen months later (August 18, 1935) Bunning died.

Bunning, Eugene McAuliffe had noted in his testimonial dinner speech, had been effective in gaining federal funds for public works projects in Rock Springs. The New Deal of President Franklin D. Roosevelt also had major impact in Rock Springs through passage in 1933 of the National Industrial Recovery Act under which the National Recovery Administration (NRA) was established. The recovery act made a difference in Rock Springs in two ways. First, it required codes of fair competition, including minimum wages and prices, in various industries, which meant coal mined in Rock Springs would no longer be penalized because it was produced under labor costs that were significantly higher than those of competitors in other states. Second, the act, in the critically influential Section 7(a), guaranteed workers freedom of choice in labor organizations. "The spark that rekindled the spirit of unionism within American labor," one historian described it. John L. Lewis used this one section of the act to revive his struggling United Mine Workers, pulling in hundreds of new members by citing Section 7(a) as evidence that "the government" recommended union membership, that "the President" wanted them to join. If no one raised any questions, the UMW organizers simply let listeners assume they meant President Roosevelt, not UMW President Lewis. The union made rapid gains in number of members but gains in hours of work each week came much slower. In a 1934 contract the miners got a seven-hour day and the thirty-five-hour week with no cut in base pay, but most mines were only working two or three days a week.

The support of the NRA was much more widespread in Rock Springs and Sweetwater County than just through the ranks of the miners' union. In a highly unionized community the pressure was on for all parts of the community to display the Blue Eagle, an emblem signifying participation in the NRA recovery plan. Harry C. Duntsch headed a drive to get signatures on a pledge to buy only at stores displaying the Blue Eagle. Duntsch was editor of the *Rocket*, which in 1931 had become a part of the chain of Wyoming newspapers being developed by Tracy S. McCraken. An assessment of the influence of the act in the county indicated that it put seven hundred men and women back to work.

After four years of austerity, the town had recovered its general sense of well-being, but that was temporarily shattered on October 29, 1935. Five boys, aged seven to twelve, were playing in vacant lots of the No. 6 district along Killpecker Creek, not far from the spot where the powder house was exploded by a pistol shot in 1891. The youngsters had with them a .22-caliber rifle, expecting to hunt rabbits, but apparently they had found only discarded pieces of junk for targets. Suddenly people in the town heard and felt the shock of an explosion. A number of adults hurried to the scene. They found a small crater in the sandy ground and shattered pieces of a greasewood bush; they found small pieces of a wooden box, which they were able to identify as a container for high explosives. They found only bits and pieces of clothing, and flesh, and bone, and they found the rifle. What happened seemed clear: one of the boys must have fired a bullet into the box he had spotted among the greasewood. Undoubtedly it had contained explosives intended for use in the mines but abandoned there below the rocky bluff west of Killpecker Creek.

Finally, at mid-decade, the U.P. Coal Company mines were working more, as many as five days in some weeks, and the railroad was reporting increased traffic. By September 1935 the U.P. Coal Company had added 500 men to the payroll bringing the total employed to 2,242—almost back to the highest figure ever—and production was up 20 percent over the previous year. In that same year the coal companies agreed to a fifty-cent-a-day increase in base pay. The economic recovery continued for Rock Springs with the U.P. mines working nearly 240 days in 1936; that was 70 percent more than the number worked in 1932. The commercial coal business was also reviving with production up 20 percent. The busy mines were consuming so much electric power the Union Pacific was forced to begin construction of a new power plant of increased capacity. The miners received another fifty-cent-a-day raise in 1937, the year in which the U.P. Coal Company became the first large coal-mining operation in the United States to be 100 percent mechanized.

About every year someone from the Union Pacific gave the influential Lions Club an update on the all-important coal business. In 1938 the speaker was a man well-known to all the members; he was George B. Pryde, newly named vice-president for the U.P. coal operations; he told the Lions the U.P. mines had produced 3,315,628 tons in 1937. Pryde, an apprentice in the mines of Scotland at the age of seven, had started his career with the Union Pacific at the No. 7 mine in 1893; by the thirties the gruff but kindly Scotsman and his family occupied the principal residence in Wardell Court, the large house at the entrance to the court.

The years 1936 and 1937 were amiable for Rock Springs in a number of ways. Even though two blustering blizzards struck in February, the weather was generally favorable, showing a remarkable record of 11.96 inches of precipitation by year's end. The previous high had been 7.65 inches in 1935. In 1937 the sheep ranches brought close to a million dollars into the area's economy with the best lamb and wool crops in fifteen years. A federally funded project made it possible for the city to widen and straighten, somewhat, the course of the Lincoln Highway along Pilot Butte Avenue. The U.P. Coal Company was nearing completion of its new huge D.O. Clark mine in Superior, where it was installing a belt conveyor system 2,600 feet long to carry the coal to the surface. Not enough unemployed youths could be found to fill the town's 1937 quota of forty for the Civilian Conservation Corps (CCC). Only eight applied. In June 1937 the North Side Catholic Church celebrated the twenty-fifty anniversary of the laying of its cornerstone with four sermons by four different ministers in one day: one sermon each in Slovak, Slovenian, Croation, and English.

In the spring of 1937 the high school basketball team won the district championship again, its fifth title in the six-year history of

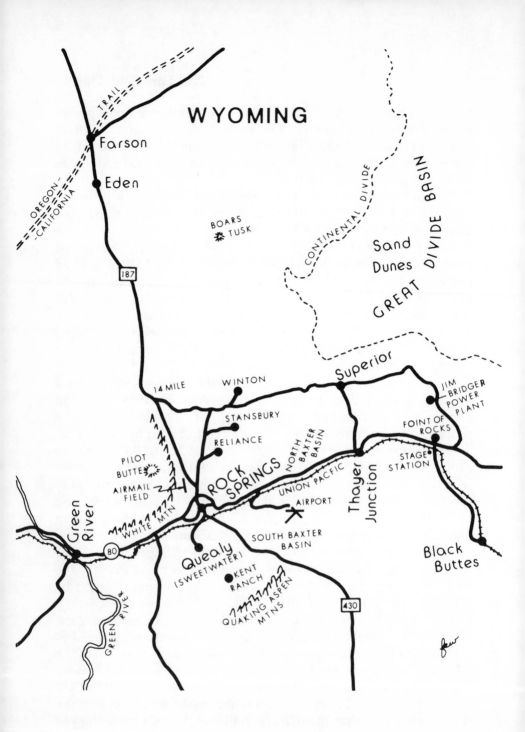

Map of the Rock Springs area. *Prepared by Frank E. Wright of Boulder, Colorado.*

the tournament in Green River, then went on to win its fifth state title as well. Between 1929 and 1937 the school's football team won the district title six times and won the state championship in 1934. All of this was accomplished with the coaching of Okie Blanchard. Then Okie announced at the end of the 1937 school year that he was leaving to be coach at the Casper High School.

Another setback for the town threatened when residents of both East Flat and West Flat were driven from their homes by another flood. This flood began Sunday, July 11, 1937, with heavy rains that overfilled usually dry Killpecker Creek, which flows from the north to join Bitter Creek near the West Flat homes. The next day cloudbursts to the east and south of town sent a bank-level wall of water down Bitter Creek from the east. Over a two-day period crews of volunteers helped city employees build dikes to hold the water surging through the creek channels. The CCC camp at Farson, established to accomplish rangeland improvements, got word of the impending disaster and rushed truckloads of youths south from the camp to help. One observer said he saw some of these young men "throw themselves into crevases being opened in the dikes and hold back the water with their bodies until sandbags were brought." The Union Pacific also closed its mines so the miners could join the battle with the water. A major flood averted, the CCC boys were invited back for a banquet prepared by a number of the town's best cooks. The next year a bond issue was approved to finance widening and straightening the creek channel.

In the 1936-1937 period hopes surged again that Rock Springs was to become a leading oil center of the West. Mountain Fuel reported a "gusher" at Powder Wash, an area miles to the southeast. The oil well, in fact, was four miles south of the Wyoming border in Colorado. The excitement ebbed as further news indicated that Powder Wash was not going to mean a boom for Rock Springs.

For substitute excitement folks strolled down to the depot to watch the new streamlined passenger trains flash through town, pulled by engines that purred loudly but never puffed. These were diesel-powered and their arrival was not good news for Rock

Springs, but their devastating impact on the town was still more than a decade away. Most locomotives on the railroad were still burning coal.

In 1938 the town's first radio station, KVRS, went on the air; programming from 6:00 to 11:00 P.M. the first day consisted entirely of local talent. At Superior the Union Pacific started production at the D.O. Clark, the "most modern coal mine in the West." It was thought this mine had tapped a coal deposit so vast, perhaps more than forty million tons, that there was little chance the town of Superior would ever become a ghost.

Also in 1938 Elmer Halseth, science and history instructor at the Rock Springs High School, kindled an interest in art by showing his classes a collection of paintings he had managed to borrow from a traveling exhibit. The students collected fifty dollars, mostly in nickels, dimes, and quarters, to buy one painting, "Shack Alley" by Henrietta Wood. Succeeding classes continued that practice and Halseth persuaded a number of persons to donate other items until Rock Springs High School had more than two hundred paintings, lithographs, and etchings, including works by Norman Rockwell, Aaron Bohrod, Grandma Moses, Peter Hurd, and such Wyoming artists as Hans Kleiber, famous for his bird etchings, and Conrad Schwiering, interpreter of the spectacular Jackson Hole landscape. Halseth then went to Washington, D.C., and got help to establish a gallery to house the collection, the Sweetwater Community Fine Arts Center, which was eventually taken over and operated cooperatively by the city of Rock Springs, Sweetwater County Library, and School District No. 1. The collection, probably worth about one million dollars by 1980, is housed in a small gallery attached to the public library and is one of the major cultural assets of the town.

10

Countdown to
the Energy Boom

One weekend late in May 1938, during the administration of Mayor Muir, the city took a count of traffic using the C Street crossing. Between 7:00 A.M. and 7:00 P.M. on that Saturday, 15,579 vehicles and 8,632 pedestrians used the crossing. The counts were smaller Sunday and Monday, but the total seemed an adequate indication of a need to do something; with the blessings and cooperation of "Uncle Pete," (the Union Pacific) the city pushed through a crossing-replacement project. Just three years later councilmen and a new mayor, Albert E. Nelson, were sitting with other local and state leaders on a temporary wooden platform near the intersection of C Street and South Front listening to Eugene McAuliffe declare Rock Springs, at long last, a "united city." Unity had been achieved by building a viaduct for vehicles over the tracks at A Street, a pedestrians-only underpass at C Street, and an underpass for both vehicles and pedestrians at M Street. The C Street surface crossing was closed and the unsightly pedestrian overpass at K Street dismantled. It was an appropriate occasion for band music, oratory, and general celebration.

By this time the city's principal means of support, the U.P. Coal Company, ranked second in Wyoming in the size of its payroll, which in 1940 totaled nearly four million dollars. The only payroll in the state that was larger was that of the coal company's parent, the U.P. railroad. Beginning in 1941 coal from the mines was being shoveled into the gigantic fireboxes of the largest steam locomotives ever built, the 4000 class 4884s. No man could shovel fast enough to fire the 150 square feet of grate in one of these

Miners with aluminum lunch pails coming off shift
and headed for the bathhouse. *Sweetwater County
Historical Society.*

monsters, so each was equipped with a mechanical stoker. These
locomotives were known as the "Big Boys," and they seemed to
foretell a long future for the coal-burning steam engine on the
U.P. line. Each locomotive weighed, when ready for the road, 350
tons, but that was about 40 percent less than the five diesel
engines needed to equal their haulage capacity. The railroad
planned to use them for towing freight trains over the mountain
country between Cheyenne and Salt Lake City, but since "Big

Boys' " could run at eighty miles an hour they were used to pull passenger trains as well.

The "Big Boys" had arrived just in time to help move an increasing load of traffic largely created by another war in Europe. With the Japanese attack on Pearl Harbor December 7, 1941, the United States was in the war. The revenues of the railroad more than doubled in the following year, and the number of working days at the mines jumped from less than two hundred in a year to more than three hundred.

Despite all this, these were troublesome years for Rock Springs. Hundreds of young men, in some cases three and even four from one family, were soon in military service, about as many volunteers as draftees. The U.P. Coal Company was plagued by a shortage of capable manpower; rationing was a constant worry, although hunters seemed to have enough gas and ammunition for frequent excursions into the country to the north; travel on the jammed and cluttered trains was uncomfortable, sometimes miserable; the town, never strongly pleasing in appearance, was visibly deteriorating; the region was largely ignored when industrial projects for the war effort were passed around; the sheepmen were in trouble as wool brought about ten cents a pound less than it cost to produce; and a coal strike in the middle of the war brought the condemnation of state and nation on the miners' heads.

In an effort to meet the demand for coal, the Union Pacific opened a new mine north of Rock Springs, near Reliance, where it could mine four seams of coal from one opening. Twelve small houses, a mine office, a shop, a warehouse, and a boardinghouse for miners in a lonely cluster on a barren, rocky hillside were the beginning of a new "company town." It was named Stansbury.

But all mines needed miners; the call to military service had cut deeply into the region's labor force. Many of the replacement miners recruited from other sections of the country either would not or could not do the work. Less than a year after the attack at Pearl Harbor, the U.P. mines were hiring women, who, after joining the union, worked mostly on picking tables in tipples, but a few were apprentice machinists, electricians, and welders in the shops. This would appear to be a clear violation of the clause in the Wyoming Constitution prohibiting women at mines except as office or clerical help. However, the company asserted it was following the dictum of the president of the United States and the chairman of the War Manpower Commission in hiring women. In any case, the company was not sued.

In October 1942 the United Mine Workers' President John L. Lewis announced that the union would ask at the expiration of contracts in April for a wage raise and other benefits, including portal-to-portal pay (paid-for-time to begin as the miner entered the mine and end as he left it). This touched off verbal attacks on Lewis as "obstructionist," "dictator," and even "traitor." He was already hated by most other labor leaders for withdrawing his union first from the AFL and then from the CIO. But the miners stuck with him for he had rebuilt their union into the most powerful and successful in the nation in 1933 and led them out of the Depression to good times and good wages. In addition, the miners believed labor was being unfairly asked to make wartime sacrifices while, they were convinced, profits of contractors and salaries of industry executives soared.

When the mine whistles sounded Saturday, May 1, 1943, normally a day of work in the mines, the miners stayed at home. Lewis did not call it a strike; he and other labor leaders had agreed to a no-strike policy after Pearl Harbor. The mines, including those in the Rock Springs area, were seized by the government and placed under the control of Secretary of Interior Harold Ickes. On Sunday, May 2, just minutes before President Roosevelt was scheduled to make a radio broadcast asking miners to go back to work, Lewis telegraphed locals across the nation ordering a return to work for a truce period so negotiations with the government could take place. When miners in the Rock Springs area, in obedience to that order, reported for work they found American flags over the mine buildings, and red, white, and blue posters announcing the mines were now "U.S. Property." When no settlement came, the miners walked out again in June, and the Wyoming Stock Growers convention passed a resolution describing the head of the UMW as "a traitor who should swing from a cottonwood tree." The miners returned once more; walked out again the twentieth of June; returned on the twenty-second, with a new deadline of October 3, 1943, for a new contract.

As negotiations for a contract continued, Eugene McAuliffe dourly predicted the worst coal shortage in history for the coming winter. His protests against what he called a short-sighted labor policy in Washington, D.C., were going unheeded while absenteeism increased among the remaining labor force in the mines, sometimes reaching as much as 20 percent of the workers on a given shift. One informal canvass of just three saloons in Rock Springs turned up eighty-seven men who should have been on shift that day. Most had been recently recruited from other areas of the nation. In addition, the turnover in the ranks of the coal miners soared to over 100 percent in a year, partly because the U.P. Coal Company was losing men lured away by higher wages in West Coast war plants.

The miners walked out again November 1, but with the government in charge they were ordered back while Lewis negotiated with the government representative, Harold Ickes. Lewis finally got virtually all he had demanded, including the pay raise and portal-to-portal pay.

For the war effort Rock Springs High School students had turned their attention to collection of newspapers, magazines, cardboard, wastepaper, and scrap metal; women prepared surgical dressings and planned menus to save sugar and shortening for the United Service Organization (USO) cookie drives. The women of Reliance sent 175 dozen cookies to the USO center at Cheyenne. Thomas Berta directed the county's war-loan bond sales, promoting the sale of bonds with personal appearances of movie stars and war heroes at his Rialto Theater, until he died in 1945. Two hundred miners voted at a union meeting to donate wages from one shift to the government for national defense. Housewives and merchants struggled to cope with the bewildering, often changing, tiny stamps and maddening paperwork of rationing. Butter all but disappeared from the grocery shelves and the cooks of Rock Springs regarded the white, lardlike oleomargarine as no substitute.

The most sought-after escape from the wartime tensions, the cinema, was often a disappointment because many movies were intended either to encourage the home front workers or exalt the fighting front heroes. Examples were *So Proudly We Hail*, starring Claudette Colbert, Paulette Goddard, and Veronica Lake as army nurses on Bataan, and *Objective Burma* in which Errol Flynn triumphed against incredible odds. More appreciated were comedies or musicals that allowed one to escape reality momentarily in laughing at Bob Hope and Dorothy Lamour as they befuddled Nazi Germany in *They've Got Me Covered* or in marveling at James Cagney's beguiling portrayal of George M. Cohan in *Yankee Doodle Dandy*.

But reality was taken seriously in Rock Springs. Claude Elias as county defense council chairman organized the area's civilian defense, including a guard unit, a control center with elaborate panel boards, and an air raid warning system, all of it rated "the most completely organized in the state." None of it was ever needed, and the city returned to peacetime pursuits at war's end in 1945.

On January 1, 1948, Wyoming General Hospital became, by act of the state legislature, Sweetwater County Memorial Hospital and under county control. In July of the same year ten nurses were graduated on the fiftieth anniversary of the nursing school. In October, the school was closed.

Late in the decade of the forties the city was dramatically reminded of one of its unsolved problems. It was after midnight January 1, 1949, as Robert H. Johnson, general manager of the *Rocket*, later to be city attorney and state senator, drove home over the A Street overpass and past the south side Catholic church. The street was deserted but several cars were parked at the church. Minutes later midnight mass ended. Young Fred Radosevich, later to be county commissioner, recalled coming out of the church with other worshippers to stare in disbelief into what seemed a bottomless pit. Most of the intersection Johnson had crossed minutes before was gone, collapsed into an abandoned mine. The city blocked off the intersection within the hour and soon after dawn began filling the gigantic hole. During the work one large dump truck and a bulldozer dropped off the crumbling edge of the hole and disappeared in the abyss. They were buried there under the rebuilt street.

Late on New Year's Day, 1949, a blizzard swept across the mountain region. The storm was not especially punishing in Rock Springs, but it did isolate the community when both ground and air transportation was halted. Eastbound trains were held in Green River for four days, then returned to Salt Lake City and routed south through Denver. On January 14 the low temperature was twenty-five below; January 15, twenty-nine below. Snowbound ranches were reached with snowplows brought from Yellowstone Park or with National Guard tracked vehicles. A brief respite in late January was followed by another blizzard early in February; trains and autos were again stalled at most towns along the Union Pacific. A thaw finally opened the highway so travel could be resumed on February 17. The U.P. mines, closed for two weeks because of the storms, resumed work February 21. About the same time trains started arriving once again from the east, with the front of some engines splattered with blood. Antelope had crowded into the railroad cuts for protection from the storm and were unable to get out of the way when the trains came through.

Another confrontation between miners and mine owners began in September 1949, and the following six months were tinged with worry and tension in Rock Springs. The walkout was not continuous, but the national union ordered a policy of working no more than three days a week at any mine that had not agreed to union terms. By February many miner's families in Rock Springs were short of food, although reports of starvation were never substantiated. However, distribution of surplus potatoes and powdered eggs and milk did bring out long lines at the Labor Temple. The annual district basketball tournament at the Green River High School gymnasium in March was interrupted momentarily when spectators took over the floor for dancing and cheering following an announcement that the union and owners had finally agreed on a settlement.

Not long thereafter the Lions Club was told that the end of

the privy in Rock Springs did not end the city's sewage problem; the problem had just moved to another part of town. The sewage disposal plant was inadequate and inefficient. A proposal for a $550,000 bond issue to build a new one hardly made the voters blink; they promptly approved it. Since the mines were working fulltime once more the economy of Rock Springs quickly revived, and the year 1953 was described by one observer as the best business year the county had ever seen. There was documentation for that in the record $28,590,000 reported in retail sales and in record high employment figures. It was a time of healthy growth, at least a minor boom.

The contribution of the coal mines to the economy that year neared $12 million, two-thirds of that payroll. The coal industry accounted for nearly one-third of the county's business activity. Another estimate suggested that coal and the railroad combined accounted for nearly one-half of all personal income earned in Rock Springs. The significance of all this was soon to be made painfully evident.

Less than three weeks before Christmas 1953 the Union Pacific Coal Company discharged 108 miners at Reliance and Hanna and not long after posted a notice on the bathhouse door at Reliance that the mine was closed. Now the full impact of the diesel locomotives that had replaced the coal burners on the railroad finally hit—hard. Miners still on the payroll in 1954 were idle many days in each month; coal production in Rock Springs that year dropped to 1,276,294 tons, less than one-half what it had been the year before and less than one-fourth of what it had been in the war years. By the end of 1954 about thirteen hundred miners had been laid off. Retail sales in the county that year managed to get above $23 million, but that was nearly a 20 percent drop from 1953. So quickly did bust follow boom. In the year 1956 for the first time in the twentieth century, coal mined in the Rock Springs area totaled less than one million tons. Would the Union Pacific soon close down its mines entirely? Company spokesmen refused to say. But there were others who were willing to predict this and dire consequences; it could mean ghost town status for Rock Springs, some thought.

From 1954 to 1957 the Union Pacific operated three mines, on a reduced scale, with a total of 500 miners at work a few days each week, at Stansbury, Superior, and at the power plant in Rock Springs. Then on a Monday in mid-February 1957, thirty-six long-time employees at the Stansbury mine received notices that they were to be transferred to Superior; no reason given, nor would U.P. officials give any explanation when questioned. Two days later in a cryptic two-paragraph notice the company announced that the Stansbury mine would be closed the following day. A copy of this notice was posted on the bathhouse door in Stansbury. The 190 still employed at the mine had worked only one day that week, and now they knew the suspense was over; they were unemployed. The last coal-burning locomotive was retired in 1958, but the company continued to mine coal part-time at Superior for about two more years, and it also operated the mine in Rock Springs near the power plant until the plant was sold to Pacific Power and Light, which brought in its own power.

The Union Pacific was an exceedingly *private* enterprise; its policies and plans were kept private. So, Mayor Edwin James was not surprised when the closing of the mines came without advance warning. The railroad's decreasing need for coal was no secret, but the complete conversion to diesel power happened earlier than planned because the railroad had an unexpected opportunity to buy a number of diesel locomotives at an especially favorable price. With this windfall, so to speak, the railroad found the coal mines a useless appendage much sooner than anticipated. The mine closings added to the burdens of the James administration at city hall, already plagued by insufficient funds, limited taxation possibilities, and a legislature's refusal to open up ways for municipalities to get more funds. In the last year of Mayor James' tenure, 1957, the city budget amounted to only $250,000.

When the census was taken in 1960, the two smallest coal camps north of Rock Springs, Winton and Dines, were gone. They were not ghost towns; they had simply vanished. The population of Reliance was down to 300, and Superior, which had 2,360 residents in 1950, had dropped to 642. The population decline in Rock Springs was less dramatic but substantial, about 500 less in

Sheep on the winter range in the Rock Springs area.
Daily Rocket-Miner Photo.

1960 than in 1950. This population decline, however, was not unique to the Rock Springs area; it was fairly general throughout Wyoming.

The future now looked bleak; pessimists were nearing a majority in Rock Springs. Nevertheless, the optimists had reasons to scoff at doomsday prophets. They sought to bolster morale, their own, perhaps, as much as anyone's, by citing cause for confidence. Sheep would help stabilize the economy. Three hundred thousand were still wintering in the area and three million pounds of wool were shipped from Rock Springs in 1954, two million of it processed in a new warehouse at Rock Springs. Sweetwater County ranked third in Wyoming in wool production, which accounted for 71 percent of the county's gross agricultural income. And what about the uranium boom? That could be something to make you forget about coal. About twenty-five hundred location notices for uranium claims were on file at the county courthouse in Green River. In addition, Mountain Fuel Supply, a company people liked to work for, with more than three hundred on its payroll was first in size in Rock Springs after the U.P. Coal Company closed its mines. It had 140 producing gas wells within a ninety-mile radius of Rock Springs and had two drill rigs working constantly. And there was still hope that someone was going to find that elusive gigantic oil field.

The most hopeful prospect of all was another mining operation that was sinking shafts nearly one-third of a mile deep about thirty miles to the west of Rock Springs. This brand-new industry in Sweetwater County had its inception about fifteen years earlier when the Mountain Fuel Supply Company drilled an exploratory well along the Black's Fork River, not far from the route Jim Bridger and Captain Stansbury had taken in 1850. Mountain Fuel was looking for gas but found none with this well. The drill bit did turn up a white substance that the company's geologist had analyzed. It was an alkali compound sometimes called sodium sesquicarbonate, soon to be popularly known in Sweetwater County as trona. This compound is a close chemical relative of sodium bicarbonate or baking soda.

The origin of the trona, geologists explain, dates from fifty million years ago when the area was covered by an inland sea. As the waters of this enormous lake rose and ebbed over thousands of years, it collected materials, varying with the different periods, that were deposited in layers at the lake's bottom. Whereas a similar process at another time and place produced massive coal deposits, in this case the results were somewhat different. There were times when the water level in the lake got very low because of prolonged evaporation. The water that was left was so heavily laden with saltlike compounds of sodium carbonates it could no longer hold them in solution and much of the salt settled to the bottom of the lake. This occurred many times and each time for a lengthy period, resulting in the layers of trona, perhaps as many as twenty-five layers, some of them twelve to fourteen feet thick, interspersed with layers of sandstone, limestone, oil shale, compacted silt, and volcanic ash. The deepest layer (the first one deposited) is believed to be about 3,500 feet below the surface and the top layer (last one deposited) at 440 feet.

Compounds of sodium carbonate are valuable, not only as the soda in the familiar yellow and red packages in kitchen and bathroom cabinets, but for making glass, paper, soap, detergents, in water softeners, and in making other chemicals. But only a Mountain Fuel Supply Company geologist got excited about mining this substance until wartime needs prompted a company known as Westvaco Corporation to make drill tests in the 1940s. It was nearly another ten years later when Westvaco finally got a shaft down and a processing plant ready so production could begin.

Trona is mined by the room and pillar method, the same as used in underground coal mines, so by the time Westvaco got its trona mine to full production it had hired about five hundred former coal miners. After the trona is brought to the surface it is heated in a kiln to remove water and then treated to remove impurities; what is left is called soda ash, which can be processed further to get bicarbonate of soda or used in manufacturing glass, and in other processes.

The Union Pacific Railroad was a partner in the emerging trona industry. Any mining done on land belonging to the railroad was bringing up trona that belonged to the railroad, and the soda ash that resulted from the processing was being shipped on the railroad. In fact, the railroad attempted to control the development of the trona industry by withholding permission to dig under even a corner of the land sections it owned, but this maneuver was defeated by an easement law passed by the state legislature.

Besides the fledgling trona industry, the optimists of Rock Springs pointed out that the U.P. Coal Company in 1957 was involved in plans for a plant that would convert some of Wyoming's vast coal deposits into liquid fuels. It was also known that construction of the Flaming Gorge Dam on the Green River southwest of Rock Springs would begin soon. As it turned out, the dam creating the Flaming Gorge Reservoir was built, but the synthetic fuel plant was not. The optimists got some help from nature in 1957 when a drought of approximately five years was finally broken with nineteen rainy days in May. Things did not seem quite so bleak as Rock Springs prepared for another municipal election that year.

Election ballots were already being prepared with the names of five candidates for mayor when a group of young men, members of the Junior Chamber of Commerce, decided to promote a write-in campaign for a sixth candidate, a young accountant named Paul Wataha. Paul protested but finally agreed, thinking there was no chance of being elected and it might be fun. He got nearly three hundred more write-in votes than his nearest competitor among the other five, whose names were all printed on the ballot. In the general election contest, Wataha won by more than a two-to-one margin. At least four factors were involved in this surprising outcome. First, his support was undoubtedly strong among the younger voters (Paul was thirty-three), among the Slavs, and among the voters generally on the north side. Second, Paul was an active member of the Democratic party, the dominant political force in Rock Springs since about 1930. Third, Paul was widely known through many civic activities: chairing the defense bond drive, promoting a Miss Rock Springs contest, active in the Junior Chamber of Commerce, on the board of the county fair, chairing the ticket committee for the first Red Desert Roundup (a rodeo), chairing the county polio drive, active with the American Red Cross chapter, president of the Jaycees, and in 1952 named the "outstanding young man of the year."

Fourth, the Wataha family had been in Rock Springs for more than seventy years. Paul's great-grandfather, a peasant from that part of the Austro-Hungarian Empire that is now Czechoslovakia and one of the first dozen or so Slavs to come to Rock Springs, was stable boss for the U.P. mines at the time of the Chinese "massacre." His grandfather, Steve Wataha, began working in the coal mines as a youngster but later was a city garbage collector. His father and mother, Mr. and Mrs. John Wataha, were widely known in the community; they seldom went out, since Mrs. Wataha, who was born in Austria, was frail and partly crippled, but they entertained often in their home near the east end of North Front Street, and their house was the unofficial head-quarters for the Democratic party. Paul's father was for years secretary of the county Democratic committee. The committee and the party caucus, as well, often met at the Wataha home over a fifth of Old Granddad. Party leaders who were guests in the Wataha home included the county commissioners, the county's state senators and representatives, Governor Lester C. Hunt, and U.S. Senator Joseph O'Mahoney. John Wataha, in addition, was nearly an institution in Rock Springs after many years at the North Side State Bank where his friendly and wise counseling won hundreds of devoted friends among the holders of small accounts. He was the north side's answer to Bob Murphy of the south side's Rock Springs National Bank. Neither man could walk down the street without encountering dozens of friendly greetings. They were the men near the centers of economic and political power with whom the average wage earner felt at ease.

On January 1, 1958, Paul, still wondering what the job involved and how it was done, took command of the municipal affairs of a city of about 10,500. A lark had turned into sober reality; he had, as he recalled it, "a city on my shoulders." Fortunately, Paul had friends who could help, particularly the former mayor, Albert E. Nelson, who agreed to serve as city attorney, and Kenneth Hamm, the police justice who was later to be district court judge. This trio was, in the beginning of Paul's lengthy tenure in the mayor's office, a sort of unofficial triumvirate, an informal cabinet, which met to discuss problems and plan strategy.

There were no overwhelming problems, but the city was losing population as men left to find jobs; the city had a bonded debt of about $800,000, mostly for the new sewage disposal plant, and the city was without funds for anything more than routine tasks. An order to fill a chuckhole in a street was only given after careful thought. The state of the city was indicated in June 1960 when the city clerk-treasurer told the city council there would barely be enough for paychecks that month. Mayor Wataha, however, regarded that situation as normal for the city, which was nearly always on the brink of being broke.

While the city administration struggled to pay its bills city residents watched the conquests of their youngsters in high school and supported a move to establish a junior college. In the spring of 1960 Rock Springs High School completed a succession of triumphs. During the school year Tiger teams had won the state football championship, the state basketball championship, the state swimming championship, the state debating championship, and two state titles in wrestling.

The same year Paul Wataha was elected mayor, 1957, Elmer Halseth, high school teacher and Sweetwater County representative in the state legislature, had called on the publisher of the *Rocket*, Dave Richardson, to suggest that Rock Springs should have a junior college. Richardson suggested that if Halseth would write a "guest editorial" he would publish it. "Why Not a Junior College Here?" Halseth headed his article in which he pointed out that junior colleges had existed for some time in other parts of Wyoming but not in the southwestern corner. Largely through Halseth's persistent efforts, the Exchange Club and the Lions Club took up the campaign, and a proposal was presented to the school board. The board chairman was Rudy Anselmi of the Miners Merc and longtime state senator from Sweetwater County. He also threw his very considerable influence behind the proposal. It was approved by voters in June 1959. The college opened with evening classes at Rock Springs High School that fall. A year later, to start a daytime program, the boards were pried off the windows and the dust swept out of the rooms in the unused school building at the onetime coal camp of Reliance, and the college classes met there until a campus atop No. 5 hill, renamed College Hill, was completed in 1969.

The college was something to be proud of but it was not an immediate or a very significant contribution to the economy.

Discouraging economic developments continued. In 1962, after the plan for processing coal into liquid fuels was abandoned, the last president of the U.P. Coal Company, Vernon O. Murray, presided over its dissolution in November. Also dissolved was the Miners Mercantile Company, the store the Anselmi family had struggled to build into a major retail market. Its old-fashioned, neighborly policies—credit; free deliveries; a discount and a treat of candy, cookies, or can of fruit when the bill was paid—were no longer competitive in a world of cut-rate supermarkets. Financial problems also forced the two Catholic schools to consolidate, although still using two buildings. The fourth, fifth, and sixth grades met at the converted Camp Pilot Butte army barracks on Elias Avenue and the primary grades at the school on A Street.

During the decade of the sixties, the major hope for an economic recovery in the area appeared to lie with the trona industry. The pioneer Westvaco plant, which had been taken over and expanded by the Food Machinery and Chemical Corporation (FMC), was joined during the decade by three others. Stauffer Chemical Company opened a mine and soda ash plant in the summer of 1962 at Big Island on the Green River, seventeen miles northwest of the town of Green River. Exploratory drilling by Texasgulf Inc. detected two beds of high-grade trona ore a few miles west of Stauffer, but mining was delayed for another decade. The fourth company in the field, Allied Chemical Company, had a mine in production not far from the original Westvaco mine in 1968, although expansion into a major operation was delayed for four years.

11

The Rise and Fall of Sin City

Tantalizing rumors spread through Rock Springs in 1969 about a major electric power plant to be built in the area, a project that would need hundreds of workers. Then, hope faded with reports that the plant might be built near Rawlins. Finally, the Pacific Power and Light Company and Idaho Power Company announced their joint venture, a huge power plant to be built by the Bechtel Corporation as prime contractor thirty-five miles east of Rock Springs on a site close to a vast seam of coal that could be strip-mined. When representatives of the plant builders held a public meeting in town to explain the plans, they said the plant, to be named for mountain man Jim Bridger, would be built in stages over several years and peak employment during construction might reach as high as 1,500 workers. About a year later the decision was made to rush construction, building all power units at one time, and employment at the construction site leaped to more than 3,000, twice the highest earlier estimate. The arrival of the first wave of this flood of temporary construction workers and their families was the first warning the town of Rock Springs had of what was coming, and before any preparations could be completed the full flood was upon the bewildered community. It was only later, after the experience of the Rock Springs boom, that the state legislature adopted rules that required advance notice to and assistance for municipalities that would be impacted by a major industrial development.

Almost simultaneously with the surge in employment at the power plant, the trona mines found increased markets for their product and began construction and hiring to double production. High wages offered at the trona mines lured many local workers but too few to fill the demand, so hundreds were recruited from other states, and about twenty families were brought from Great Britain. The amount of trona mined jumped from 4 million tons in 1970 to 8.8 million tons in 1976, and 11 million tons in 1977. Processing in the plants at the mines produced refined soda ash equal to about two-thirds of the tonnage of the raw trona. This product was shipped via the U.P. railroad in specially designed cars to glass and chemical plants in the East, or to ports on the West Coast for shipment to Japan. A small part of it was processed into baking soda (sodium bicarbonate) by a Church & Dwight plant near the Allied Chemical mine and sold under the Arm & Hammer brand name.

In 1977 employment in the Sweetwater County trona industry had surged to about 3,700. Most of those workers commuted from Green River; only about one-fourth lived in Rock Springs. Although the trona companies annoyed public officials by not giving advance warning of the spectacular expansion that brought in a flood of new employees, the companies did buy, lease, or construct employee housing, mostly in Green River, which, as a consequence, jumped from a population of less than 5,000 in 1970 to nearly 13,000 in 1980.

Added to all this was an oil boom. Activity by drilling rigs searching for deposits of oil and gas had been increasing throughout much of Wyoming since 1973 when the oil producing countries of the Middle East slapped on an oil embargo and the Organization of Petroleum Exporting Countries (OPEC) quadrupled oil prices. The resulting "energy crisis" magnified the rush to find all and any energy sources. Wyoming, as the state's U.S. Senator Gale W. McGee pointed out, was one of the nation's greatest potential sources of energy and minerals. Surveys indicated that in addition to containing 30 percent of the nation's uranium ore reserves, Wyoming ranked fourth among the fifty states in coal reserves, among the top five states in crude oil reserves, and among the top seven in gas reserves.

This was not news to the oil companies. They were already

rushing drilling rigs and crews into the state, many headed for the Overthrust Belt, a forty-mile wide strip of rugged land that runs hundreds of miles north and south, with many curves and bows, from Canada to Mexico. This belt was formed millions of years ago when two continental land plates collided, and one thrust itself over the other, in the process forming traps for oil and gas with production potential second only to Prudhoe Bay, Alaska. Part of the Overthrust Belt stretches along the western border of Wyoming. The complex geology of this area plus the need to drill down 10,000 feet or more had discouraged exploration until prices of those energy treasures suddenly tripled and quadrupled.

The major impact of the rush to the Overthrust Belt struck the town of Evanston, but there was significant drilling activity in the Rock Springs area as well, particularly in the Brady oil field and Patrick Draw. Almost overnight oil well service companies, some with a half dozen employees, others with three dozen or more, moved into town and added a new phrase to the vocabulary of townfolk, "oil patch," to refer to a stretch of Elk Street north of downtown where these companies set up their headquarters.

Others in the frantic rush to get rich on unexploited energy sources in Wyoming were after uranium or coal. Uranium was thought to be plentiful in low-grade deposits in the state, and low grade now had high value with uranium prices up about five times. Coal, it had been known for years, was Wyoming's most plentiful energy resource, and with the oil embargo it appeared the nation would have to return to a heavy reliance on coal. New mines were opened up, including the Black Buttes strip mine east of Rock Springs along the route of the Overland stagecoach line and the strip mine at the Jim Bridger power plant.

The sixty square miles of the Black Buttes mine make it one of the largest surface coal mines in the United States. Production was started there in 1979 by Peter Kewitt Sons in partnership with Rocky Mountain Energy Company, the U.P. railroad subsidiary. One of the coal seams at this mine was reported to be twenty-six feet thick. The company built a conveyor belt three and one-half miles long to move the coal from the mine to the railroad spur where a slowly moving train of 100 cars can be loaded with 10,000 tons of coal in two hours.

The Bridger mine was connected with the power plant by a seventy-foot-wide highway for the gigantic coal haulers that carried 110 tons in a single load at speeds of more than forty miles an hour. In 1977 the power plant consumed five million tons from a coal mine that could eventually be 4,000 feet wide and ten miles long.

Inevitably, with all this activity bringing new workers and their families into the area, one other thing happened. Rock Springs of the 1970s in some respects was once again a frontier town, repeating the excesses that had been characteristic of the "Hell on Wheel" towns of the 1860s during the construction of the transcontinental railroad. Just as moths cannot resist the attraction of a light, denizens of the underworld cannot resist a boom town. No one ever got an accurate count of how many of these modern day "camp followers" added themselves to the crowds in Rock Springs. They were the most temporary of all, like moths fluttering about by night, and mostly under the lights on K Street and Pilot Butte Avenue.

A period of rapid expansion was nothing new to Rock Springs; it had experienced its first boom in the second decade of its existence and survived a number of boom-bust cycles thereafter. It was the magnitude and the momentum of this explosive boom in the first half of the 1970s that made it such a staggering blow to the town. The mathematics of this boom are mind-boggling; its impact on the human beings in the community was mind-numbing. First the figures.

The U.S. census of 1970 listed the population of Rock Springs as 11,657. Estimates of the population only four years later ranged from a low of 20,000 to a high of 26,000. The disparity is probably explained by two factors: the highly mobile nature of the new population and variations in the total area covered by the different estimates. Some people tried to add up the total number of new workers in this wave of sojourners from Texas, Oklahoma, Louisiana, California, Washington, Illinois, and several other states, attracted to Rock Springs "for the big bucks;" one estimate was 6,000—in a town that three or four years earlier had a total population of less than 12,000! Add in families brought by some, but not all, of the imported workmen, and the estimated population of Rock Springs was clearly above 20,000, and a 26,000 estimate may have been closer to the mark. The population of the county had also more than doubled from 18,391 in 1970 to an estimated 45,000 by 1975.

Despite the rapid rise in the labor force from this unprecedented in-migration, unemployment was, according to the director of the Wyoming State Employment Office, Ernie Mecca, "negligible," less than one-half of one percent. Old-timers were aghast to hear the wages being earned on the new jobs; mere youngsters were getting $40 a day "just for common labor!" And getting travel pay, to boot, for the thirty-five miles to the Bridger power plant site. Skilled tradesmen, electricians, pipefitters, carpenters, were getting about twice as much. It was estimated in 1974 that the average salary in Rock Springs was $9,688, which took into account the relatively low pay of schoolteachers, store clerks, janitors, and others. The high incomes of the boom years were probably more accurately reflected in Internal Revenue Service figures, which showed taxpayers of the Rock Springs zip code area (829) as the fifth wealthiest in the nation with a median adjusted gross per capita income of $17,389 in 1979, and the wealthiest of all in 1982 at $23,230!

Retail business in Rock Springs totaled $48 million in 1970; it jumped to $75 million by 1975. In 1971 the total number of licenses to do business in Rock Springs was five hundred; in the next four years that total more than doubled. In the preboom year of 1970 the city issued sixty-five building permits; the annual average for several subsequent years was ten times that figure. The number of new sewer hookups in 1970, seventy-five; in the immediate years thereafter, nine hundred each year! The city budget of $671,000 in 1970 rocketed to a figure almost twelve times as large—$8 million—in 1977!

Enrollment in the schools increased by 50 percent between 1970 and 1974. A junior high school designed for 800 was bulging with 1,200 before a new building could be completed. Not only did new faces arrive in the schoolrooms at a bewildering pace, many of them disappeared almost before teachers could connect face with name. By the time records from previous schools arrived, some of the new pupils were already gone.

In 1970 the dispatchers at the police radio room logged 9,000 calls. In 1973 the figure was more than 100,000.

This overwhelming magnitude of the boom crushed the original welcoming anticipation that followed the first news of the plan for the Jim Bridger plant. Initially the plant seemed, to some at least, a dream come true. Rock Springs people like most Wyomingites wanted development of the resources in a state that, in their view, had been largely ignored and development starved for more than a century. But the dream turned out to be a nightmare of social and environmental disaster that threatened to wreck their way of life.

Genuine Wyomingites, native or transplanted, have a strong affection for the limitless outdoors where they find, not emptiness, but a glorious sense of freedom, where, as Dick Randall of Rock Springs once expressed it, they can experience "the wonderful therapy provided by a sparkling trout stream," or where at night when the thousands of stars make no noise they can feel the soft engulfing embrace of silence. The invading "horde," which included many who wanted to try the hunting and fishing, seemed a threat to Sweetwater County wildlife: pronghorn antelope, sagebrush elk, bald and golden eagles, sage grouse, howdy-do owls, white-tailed prairie dogs, and wild horses. In addition, for a time it seemed there was another endangered species, the Rock Springs native.

On the other hand, most newcomers found Rock Springs a disappointment. They had heard about wide open spaces, but few expected an empty hundred miles of it in all directions. They had imagined, perhaps, a peaceful mountain valley (after all the elevation of Rock Springs is above 6,000 feet) with pine-covered slopes and a trout-laden, bubbling stream. The reality was a shock that probably contributed heavily to the 60 to 80 percent job turnover in the area during the seventies.

So for both newcomers and natives the reality of the boom as opposed to the dream was a backwash of headaches and frustrations, of disappointment and disillusionment, which stemmed in part from the crowds of strangers in restaurants, bars, grocery stores, and post office. Pilot Butte Avenue, Bridger Avenue, Center Street, Elk Street—all were chocked with cars and pickup trucks; most seemed to have out-of-state licenses. One veteran teacher in the area, Louise Pryde (nearly everyone called her Judy), said, "We have just one problem: people pollution."

The effects of all this were many and varied but mostly distressful. What had been a strong sense of community was seriously weakened, some thought destroyed. One puzzled resident commented about "discontent" and people complaining. "I don't remember people complaining before," she said. Many said the town's traditional friendliness was gone. Long-time residents perceived the town as taken over by newcomers; newcomers perceived the town as unfriendly and lacking in "things to do." Natives in service jobs around town found themselves suddenly on the bottom of an inflated pay scale; the newcomers were making the big salaries. Some natives, of course, quit their low-paying jobs and went to the power plant or trona mines to get in on the bonanza. Those that stuck it out in their old jobs, schoolteachers, for example, were soon struggling to cope with an inflated cost of living. Businessmen, too, were pinched. They lost many employees to the new higher-paying jobs, often couldn't find replacements, and couldn't afford to pay enough to attract replacements if they were available.

People in charge of businesses or public offices felt overwhelmed by the problems, lacked understanding of the full nature of what was happening, and had woefully inadequate resources for coping, even if they figured out how. Some of the new people had answers, they thought, based on "how we did it back home," an attitude often resented by the natives. The increase in stress was universal. As a result the caseload at the mental health center increased ninefold in the first five years of the boom, and that was caused mostly by long-term residents, not newcomers. But the stress was notable on the newcomers as well, who were living lonely and barren lives in what they perceived as a lonesome and barren land. There was a difference between the

A coal seam was exposed when part of a hill was sliced away above a mobile home court on the southeast edge of Rock Springs. Dozens of such courts were established during the boom of the seventies. *Photo by Author.*

harried homemaker in the dugout on Bitter Creek in 1875 and her successor in the crowded trailer in 1975; but there were similarities, too. Both struggled with dust, mud, inadequate water and disposal systems, fussing children, and a pestering wind.

A city that in the past had managed with a minimum amount of zoning and planning was suddenly overwhelmed by a host of problems, all needing immediate attention and most needing an infusion of money the city did not have and had little prospect of getting. The first problem was housing. An early estimate as the boom developed indicated a need for 920 short-term housing units; that turned out to be more than 2,000 short of the reality. It was a bonanza for those with houses for sale or rent. A house for sale in 1970 for $24,000 got no takers; in 1973 the same house sold readily at $32,000. Eventually about one-half of the population lived in trailers or mobile homes. Because building for the long term was foolish when many of the new residents expected to stay only briefly, trailers or mobile homes seemed a reasonable solution. Also, a few hundred found housing in the nearby ex-coal camps of Reliance and Superior, giving both new life, and parked trailers and mobile homes more than tripled the size of the tiny settlement at Point of Rocks, once the site of a stage station

Before long there were few spots left in the trailer parks, and fees for those few were high, so newcomers simply picked a convenient flat spot amidst the sagebrush for parking a camper or pitching a tent. One Rock Springs resident on a drive over the ten-mile road from Point of Rocks to the Bridger power plant counted three hundred temporary dwellings—trailers, campers, tents and even a few sheep-herder wagons, squatting in the sagebrush along the road. These temporary camps were occupied for the summer only, and many of them by college students intent on saving all wages possible over the summer. A few employees at the power plant commuted by airplane from Craig, Colorado, or Riverton, Wyoming.

The second major problem that plagued the city was the need to expand basic municipal services: police and fire protection, water supply, sewage disposal, recreational facilities, and streets for increased traffic. The need for improvements in all these areas was immediate, but there was no way to get immediate funding. By law in Wyoming, facilities cannot be taxed until they are operational; the first power unit of the Bridger plant only became operational in 1973. Medical services, modest at best before the boom, were by 1974 grossly inadequate; most of the six primary care physicians in town were no longer accepting new patients. The only place for many to get medical help was at the hospital emergency room, which treated sixteen thousand persons during 1973, an average of nearly forty-five patients a day.

The school district, trying to deal with the burgeoning enrollment, finally got a $5.3 million bond issue passed but ballooning construction costs ate up a large part of this before planned buildings could be erected. The district did get a junior high school built and one elementary school, but two other elementary schools, a swimming pool, and planned renovations had to be dropped.

The downtown section, North and South Front streets and adjacent areas, was rapidly turning into a depressed district, largely abandoned by shoppers in favor of new stores that had popped up in a shopping district on the west side. Buildings in the old district were run down, needed repair; but property owners complained that they could not afford to renovate or remodel when rents were so low, and rents could not be increased because the business had gone to the new outlying shopping center. In addition, the downtown area was plagued by subsidence. Why should an owner fix up a building that might tomorrow drop into the excavated mine beneath it? A Downtown Merchants Association was formed but it found no solutions.

Midway through the decade of the seventies, about the time that the boom hit its peak and began to decline, solutions began to catch up with some of the problems. To build a "beltway" for traffic to go around to the south of the city, instead of through the bottleneck of Pilot Butte Avenue, the city borrowed $5.2 million from the State Farm Loan Board, then went to the Wyoming Community Development Group and asked it to repay the Farm Loan Board out of coal tax revenue.

The state finally agreed to return one-third of the three-cent sales tax to the cities, twice what the cities had been getting, and also allowed a local-option additional one-cent sales tax to meet local needs if approved by popular vote. This extra tax must be re-approved by voters every two years. Sales tax revenue in 1970 for Rock Springs had been $160,000; in 1976 it was $2,800,000.

With this increased income the city was able to accomplish a number of things. One was an expanded sewage disposal plant. The plant of the 1950s, which had been declared by state health officials to be "one of the best—if not the best—in the state," was functioning at less than capacity in 1970; two years later it was overburdened. Raw sewage was being dumped into Bitter Creek in a malodorous reminder of the town's early history as a coal camp. By the time the new plant was finished, the boom was over. The construction crew at the Bridger power plant had been cut in half by 1975.

The increase in funds also allowed a return to one of Mayor Wataha's favorite projects, a major recreational complex. Land north of the city was selected for the project, and a golf course, club house, tennis courts, and ball fields planned. Foolishness, some people said. The grass will never grow; the trees will blow over; and golfers will watch their golf balls being blown off over the hills to Superior. But, with the help of the sales tax money, by the 1980s there was an expanse of fairways below White Mountain, a startling green oasis where once there had been only sagebrush, greasewood, and saltbush. The unsquelchable golfers of Sweetwater County now for the first time had a course with grass fairways and greens, a handsome course, the dream of such golfers as Art Taucher, who won a bronze medal on National Golf Day in 1952 by shooting a net 70 on the rocky fairways and oiled sand "greens" of the old Dead Horse Canyon links to beat Ben Hogan's 71 on a real grass course in Dallas, Texas.

In a further effort to turn the boom into bloom, plans were made to extend this beautification to other areas, with the women's clubs struggling to help the city's Cleanup and Beautification Committee. The chairperson was Dorothy Worrall, wife of Kenneth Worrall, who was employed at the Bridger power plant. The city began in the late seventies to expand its acreage of parks and continued this campaign into the eighties. A number of grass-covered neighborhood parks were established and trees, grass, and shrubs were planted along Dewar Drive in the neighborhood of the west-end shopping center. Now there were no *Keep Off the Grass* signs. The Chamber of Commerce had available a car bumper sticker which read: Rock Springs — Bringing Beauty to the Desert.

After sixteen plus years in the mayor's office, the last two and one-half during the bruising boom, Paul Wataha did not file for reelection in 1974. It didn't matter; another write-in campaign returned him to the office anyway for another four-year term. During the first two years of this term it appeared that the city might be getting control of at least some of its problems. Some relief was in sight for the schools; the city would be getting some

The Union Merc sign still hangs from the building at the corner of Fifth and K streets, but the space is actually being used by a pool room. Across the street is the OK Bar. *Photo by Author.*

significant help from the change in the taxing laws and from new funds established by the state; the employment at the power plant dropped more than 50 percent as construction there neared completion.

But one particularly nagging problem that still remained was an undermanned police force that was not dealing effectively with the crowd of gamblers, pimps, prostitutes, and various criminal types that infested the town. The bars and many restaurants were crowded and raucous every night and doubly so on weekends. Long-time residents were avoiding most of the bars and some of the restaurants, especially those on K Street, where on weekends the prostitutes patrolled, some said, in platoons. Some residents insisted they were afraid to go downtown.

City officials cited the loading records of airplanes landing at the Rock Springs airport on Fridays and departing on Sundays to support their assertion that the prostitutes were mostly "circuit hookers" flown in from Colorado Springs and Salt Lake City for the weekend trade. "It was a different bunch of girls each weekend," one said. Mayor Wataha and the city attorney, Robert H. Johnson, appealed to the FBI for help in curbing this traffic across state lines, but were told "we're too busy to deal with that."

Some merchants on K Street, other than the bar owners, said this underworld infestation ruined their businesses by driving away their regular customers. The Union Mercantile, which had modernized and expanded its establishment on the corner of K and Fifth streets in an effort to compete with new supermarkets, finally gave up the struggle and closed for good in 1978. At one of the most popular restaurants on this street, the New Grand, the proprietor, Sonny Leo, found his old clientele largely replaced by boisterous crowds of workers from the oil patch and the power plant construction site. He said one of his major problems was created by the prostitutes, who walked through the cafe propositioning men sitting at the tables. He ordered them out, but they only cursed him. Sometimes he locked the front door to keep them out. Calling the police, he said, did no good; sometimes the police never came, or if they did they were too late to deal with the problem. The harassed policemen, however, believed that some incidents were created on the infamous K Street to occupy the forces of law and order so robberies or other activities could take place unmolested in other parts of town.

Many persons believed, with some justification, that at least a few of the police were involved in the criminal activity. One patrolman, in a scene that might have come from a grade B movie, met surreptitiously with two men he presumed were organized crime figures to offer his help (for a share of profits) in taking control of the drug traffic and prostitution in Rock Springs. It turned out the men were undercover police agents.

In an effort to improve the police force, Wataha hired a former police officer, Clyde Kemp, in the spring of 1977 as safety director to supervise both police and fire departments. Kemp lasted just three months. He said he resigned because his "clean-up" efforts were blocked; Wataha said Kemp had the police department in such "disarray we had to do something." Shortly before that the director of the state's criminal investigation division, Neil Compton, was fired by Wyoming Governor Ed Herschler. Compton and Kemp both charged they were victims of an attempt to cover up corruption in high places. To probe these claims a state grand jury was formed in the fall of 1977.

Meanwhile the mass media got interested. Reporters from newspapers in Casper, Cheyenne, Denver, Salt Lake City, Los Angeles, from *Newsweek, Time,* and the broadcasting networks arrived and quickly had Rock Springs labeled as the modern-day Sodom or Gomorrah, the nation's "sin city," a rest and recreation center for criminals. One magazine stated flatly that ex-cop Clyde Kemp was fired for "doing too much good" and that top city officials might soon be indicted on corruption charges. None were. "The best guess is," reported another, that "many of the city's leaders and some state officials" were involved in "wide-open vice." A Dan Rather two-part report on the CBS "60 Minutes" program in the fall of 1977, was the capping journalistic performance. Viewers watched a murky television screen as Rather said "hookers openly work the streets and the bars." The shots, taken with a special night lens, showed scenes on K Street, which Rather reported was "steeped in prostitution, gambling, and narcotics." He added, "Vice runs rampant and a handful of men run the city as they please." Much of the "60 Minutes" programs was based on assertions by Compton and Kemp. Prostitution was nothing new on K Street; it had existed there for a century, but never quite so openly, and never before with so many practitioners.

The grand jury probing went on for a year, leaving a city tense and divided, individuals fearful and suspicious of being "set up," but never produced any charges against any public official in Rock Springs or Sweetwater County. The jury's report did say that "wide open and well organized" prostitution and gambling existed in Rock Springs beginning in 1973 "with little interference from local law enforcement . . . until some time late in 1977." Unidentified witnesses, evidently police officers, had told the jury that when efforts were made to clamp down on the vice operations "superiors" told them to give their time to more important things. The jury found no evidence of payoffs or bribes, but its report added: "It is, nevertheless, puzzling why this illegal activity could go on as it did." City officials, in reply, suggested that they had gone as far as they thought they could without risking charges of violating civil rights: "We couldn't arrest people because they looked like prostitutes or pimps."

Paul Wataha and others connected with his city administration at the time insist that the barrage of reports of corruption in Rock Springs "was a politically motivated attack" designed to discredit the Democratic party and some of its leaders in the state before the election of 1978, the twenty-first and last year Wataha served as mayor of Rock Springs. Because of the published or broadcast speculations about corruption in his city administration, Wataha filed libel suits against a half dozen corporations or individuals. All were either settled out of court or dropped. Wataha said he dropped his suit against CBS and Dan Rather because of his health; he had suffered a heart attack, which he believed was brought on by stress.

The uproar left much of the nation wondering about this "awful place in Wyoming," where, in fact, most Rock Springs residents still pursued as best they could lives that were law abiding, hard working, and socially responsible. But the grand jury probing had one tragic but unintended consequence that seemed to justify *Oui* magazine's characterization of Rock Springs as "one of the meanest town's in America," and assertions that it was still a hangout for outlaws as it was in the days of Butch Cassidy and the Wild Bunch, a haven for wild and uninhibited survivors of the old Frontier West.

The man who succeeded Kemp as Rock Springs' director of

public safety was Sweetwater County Undersheriff Ed Cantrell, who at age fifty was a veteran law enforcement officer with a reputation for toughness, honesty, and the skill of an old-time, western gunfighter, able to draw and fire his revolver in two-tenths of a second. Cantrell took charge of a police department that had just fifteen policemen shortly before the "60 Minutes" program was aired and while the grand jury probe was going on. Years later Cantrell told an interviewer: "You didn't try to police Rock Springs back then. You just tried to survive."

One of Cantrell's first decisions was to hire a twenty-nine-year-old Puerto Rican undercover narcotics agent from New York City, Michael Rosa, whose operations in Rock Springs eventually resulted in seventeen arrests the following spring. After that Rosa seemed unhappy, difficult to get along with. Friday, July 14, 1978, the newspapers reported that three Rock Springs police officers, including Rosa, had been subpoenaed to appear before the grand jury in Cheyenne. Cantrell and others on the police force wondered why Rosa had been called. Was it about a mix-up in the records concerning Rosa's expenses? It seems Rosa didn't know why he had been summoned either, although he, too, was apparently worried about the expense voucher business. Or maybe he feared that the grand jury was believing rumors that he was actually involved in the drug business himself. Or did he carry a secret about the suspected corruption in Rock Springs? His wife said he remarked as he left on Saturday night to go to the Silver Dollar bar on North Elk Street: "If I don't come back tonight, don't feel bad. I'm getting into some things that could put people higher up behind bars."

Cantrell and two of his police staff were driving about discussing the situation that night when Cantrell told the man behind the wheel of the unmarked police car to drive to the Silver Dollar and to radio the police dispatcher orders to call Rosa at the bar and tell him to meet them out in front of the bar. Cantrell said later he wanted to find out from Rosa "what was going on."

Cantrell was in the passenger side of the front seat; Rosa, when he came out of the bar carrying a plastic wineglass, got in the back seat behind the driver. He shoved the glass between his legs.

"What do you motherfuckers want?" he asked.

A moment later there was a blast from a gun and Rosa was dead, from a .38-caliber bullet that had struck between his eyes slightly to the left of the bridge of his nose.

"He was coming at me," Cantrell said. "I seen it in his eyes." Then he handed his gun over to the officer driving the car and waited.

Cantrell testified at his trial for murder in November 1979 that he had his hand on his pistol, tucked under his belt in front, when Rosa got into the car. Rosa, staring at Cantrell, threw his head and shoulders back.

Cantrell said, "I thought, 'No, oh, no!' Then I shot him."

Rosa's gun never got out of its holster.

Cantrell convinced Gerry Spence, a Wyoming lawyer well known for his work in a number of sensational trials, that he had shot in self-defense, so Spence agreed to defend him in court. Spence brought witnesses to the stand who testified that Rosa was a drug user and had supplied others with drugs. With Spence's help Cantrell also convinced the trial jury of the validity of his self-defense claim and he went free—of prison, but not free of the suspicion held by a great many that he had gotten away with murder. Cantrell, Spence, and others blamed pretrial news reporting that, they said, convicted him in advance, for the undying suspicion that continued to haunt Cantrell long after the trial.

Reminders of the early coal town years are still visible in Rock Springs. A remnant of the Fountain Club sign still exists on a South Front Street building, seen here between the cars of a U.P. freight train. The space once occupied by a popular saloon was being used by a pet shop in 1986. *Photo by Author.*

12

The Sinking City

After the trial Cantrell did not return to his job as director of public safety at Rock Springs; the city abolished that position. Cantrell wandered aimlessly for a while, drinking too much, then was hired by the livestock men in southwestern Wyoming to ride the range hunting rustlers. Although he brought no one in for trial on rustling charges, the stockmen said he was effective. When would-be rustlers learned Ed Cantrell, whom Gerry Spence called the last of the great gunfighters, was patrolling the southwestern Wyoming rangelands, they looked for opportunities elsewhere.

Wataha again declined to file for reelection and this time, probably to his relief, there was no draft by way of a write-in campaign. Rightly or wrongly (a matter of often vigorous dispute), his administration had been largely discredited by the sensations of the "60 Minutes" program and the Rosa slaying with the succeeding Cantrell trial. Stunned by the Rosa affair, the people of Rock Springs desperately wanted a cleansing, a reform that would repair the reputation of their town. Keith West, owner of a petroleum distribution business, was elected mayor in 1978 on a promise to bring about a cleanup and reform, but it was time that provided healing, to a considerable extent, although a *Denver Post* reporter thought credit was due "reformist Keith West . . . and his hard-driving police chief, Russ Hawk."

While the excitement of the Rosa killing and the Cantrell trial claimed the center of attention, the underworld of K Street and the economy of the region began to shrink back to preboom proportions. The construction workers at the power plant left for jobs elsewhere, and the boom in the trona business began to fade.

Rock Springs remained true to its historical pattern; it was on a downward economic curve again. While the rest of the nation slid into a mild recession, the Rock Springs boom simply collapsed. The story was told by the economic reports of the Sweetwater County Planning Department. Among other things these reports showed employment in the county plunged from a high of 23,203 in 1981 to 18,000 in 1984, a 22 percent decline. The deepest drops were in mining and construction. By June 1983 the unemployment rate in the county was 11.6 percent but from then until the following June the number of active job seekers dropped by 35 percent as people left the area to look for work. In Rock Springs housing of any kind had been virtually unobtainable in the 1970s, there were vacancies ranging as high as 30 percent. In Green River residential building permits issued in 1981 totaled 319; in 1984 the total was 84. When sales tax collections dropped 26 percent statewide, they plunged nearly 38 percent in Sweetwater County. But betting on the horse races at the thirty-day season at the county fair track north of Rock Springs remained steady.

There were three major contributing factors to the slump in Sweetwater County. First was a major shrinkage in the market for soda ash. State Department of Labor Statistics show that employment in the trona industry dropped nearly 25 percent between 1981 and 1985. In addition, the trona miners still employed agreed to new no-raise contracts. Trona production began a serious plunge in mid-1982 primarily because of a decline in the demand for new glass; a major factor was increased use of containers fashioned from aluminum, plastic, or recycled glass. Thirty glass manufacturing plants east of the Mississippi River closed between 1978 and 1985. Clear evidence of the trona slump was provided by the long lines of empty trona cars left standing month after month on the U.P. railroad sidings in Green River and east of Rock Springs.

A second contributor to the recession in Rock Springs was the drying up of the oil patch. At the peak of the drilling boom for oil and gas, there were more than two hundred rigs at work in Wyoming early in 1982. One year later, after an abatement of the oil crisis, there were about one-fourth that many in the state. This was also partly caused by a decline in the demand for natural gas. Following a change in federal law that encouraged exploration by allowing high prices for newly discovered gas, drilling expanded; then supplies soared, but the high prices continued; so consumers cut back on consumption, and the market was shattered. In 1983 about 400 of 1,800 wells were "shut in," capped until markets improved. When most of the drilling rigs departed, the demand for service and tools collapsed; the result was a rash of bankruptcies and vacancies along Elk Street, once the oil patch of Rock Springs.

The recession punctured the demand for electrical power as well, and as a result the Bridger power plant was operated in 1983 at one-half of capacity; only two of the four five-hundred-megawatt units were in operation, and this resulted in layoffs at the coal mine. In general the Rock Springs area never did see the predicted boom in coal production because of the energy crisis. One reason was shipping cost. Eighty-four percent of Wyoming coal is shipped out of state by rail, and the transportation cost drove the price of the coal up between 35 and 70 percent. It was cheaper for coal consumers in coastal areas to buy imported coal brought in by ship. A number of Wyoming coal mines were closed, but owners tried to keep their state permits updated so that they could resume production if conditions altered.

As the state and the Rock Springs area were struggling to recover from the recession, they suffered another humiliating defeat when Amtrack decided to pull its passenger trains off the Union Pacific tracks and send them by a more scenic route over the Rocky Mountains via the Rio Grande tracks between Denver and Salt Lake City. Protests and threats of court suits were of no avail. The one-time "Hell-on-Wheels" railroad camps of southern Wyoming, which struggled to maturity as cities, were without railroad passenger service for the first time in their history. In addition, the Rock Springs airport, once served by United Airlines flights, and then by Frontier, by 1984 found itself left with only commuter service from Salt Lake City and Denver.

In 1983 many parts of Wyoming were showing economic improvement, but Sweetwater County was lagging until nearly

1985 when employment surged again with the start of new construction projects, including new work at the Bridger power plant and construction at the hospital and junior college. Two new major plants were also started; one near the southern limits of the city was the Chevron Chemical Company's phosphate fertilizer plant, which began operating in 1986.

The second plant, an Exxon project, was being constructed about a two-hour commuting ride northwest of Rock Springs. This plant, where construction began in the spring of 1984, was to process natural gas from wells along the eastern edge of the Overthrust Belt. The gas contains about 70 percent carbon dioxide, and the Exxon plant is intended to extract this gas to be used for increasing the output from oil wells. The carbon dioxide is pumped into the ground near oil wells, and the pressure of the gas forces unretrieved oil to the surface. Other parts of the gas extracted from the Riley Ridge wells—methane, hydrogen sulfide, nitrogen, and helium—Exxon also expected to capture for commercial uses. Approximately 50 percent of the construction workers on this plant were already residents of southwestern Wyoming, many from Rock Springs. Some of the families of workers hired from other areas made their homes in Rock Springs, but the impact on Rock Springs of the Exxon plant was only a fraction of what the town had experienced during the Bridger power plant construction. Also, new state laws born of the Rock Springs experience in the seventies required new plants to provide specific assistance to nearby communities in meeting the demands of increased population.

In the eighties rather than being called "sin city," Rock Springs was being referred to as the "sinking city," because of increased incidents of subsidence. Over a period of at least eighty years, the ground had displayed a frightening tendency to collapse into the abandoned mine excavations under about nine hundred acres of the city. That included sixty-three miles of a network of tunnels and rooms in the No. 1 mine alone. City hall did not have a complete record of all the cases of subsidence, but there seemed to be little doubt that they numbered over the years more than one hundred.

Cases were reported early in the twentieth century, including one incident in which a twelve-year-old boy, romping across a vacant lot between A and Walnut streets, suddenly disappeared, as though swallowed up by the earth. As it turned out, such was the case. A playmate gave the alarm and rescuers discovered a hole, about three feet in diameter and twenty-five feet deep, created when the earth collapsed into a room of the abandoned U.P. No. 2 mine. George Rodda, unhurt at the bottom, was rescued with a length of rope.

A number of cave-ins occurred along North Front Street and South Front and under or near the railroad tracks, including the one that created a massive hole in front of the south side Catholic church in 1949. The railroad had tried to fill in the voids under the tracks in the thirties and again in the forties, but the subsidence cases continued, causing a minor train derailment in 1982. Starting in 1976, damage so severe that houses had to be abandoned occurred in south-central Rock Springs in the area of Connecticut and New Hampshire streets, near the Mountain Fuel Company office building. Residents reported hearing loud "popping" noises and then discovered foundations had dropped away from walls.

Investigations convinced the city engineer's office that most of the subsidence cases occur in areas where the depth of the ground between the roof of the mine and the land surface above is no more than about 120 feet. Subsidence occurs when a few feet of the clay ceiling of the excavation collapses to the mine floor, leaving an arching cavity; later that process repeats as the new roof of the cavity collapses, and keeps repeating until it reaches the surface.

What were the possible solutions? The surest action would be to pour in great quantities of cement to fill up the voids, but that would be prohibitively expensive. A substitute might be to pour in a slurry mixture of sand or crushed rock and water to backfill the tunnels and thus prevent collapse. For spots where a collapse had already occurred, grouting was a possibility; this involved pumping grout, a mortarlike material, into the voids to form a supporting column that would take a roughly pyramidal shape.

After the city finally persuaded the state and federal government to take the problem seriously enough to offer financial help, the question became what to do. The slurry method was adopted in the residential area near the Mountain Fuel offices. Then correction effort began full speed in 1985 with grouting in the downtown area and the sand and slurry method along Ridge Avenue, north side, and along Adams Avenue, south side.

But suddenly there were anguished cries from homeowners one block west of Adams, along McKinley Avenue, where houses were suddenly exhibiting new cracks. The residents there blamed the problem on the slurry injections. Mrs. Mary Rynio became leader of a committee of homeowners determined to stop the backfilling of the mine. That was fitting, because she had had to move out of a home on Adams Avenue because of subsidence and now she lived on McKinley. The work was halted for investigations. The slurry, it was found, tended to form dams underground that blocked its flow through the mine tunnels, then as more was pumped down, it began to seek outlets elsewhere and this could have been causing ground shifts in adjacent areas. The backfilling injections were abandoned.

Other problems developed elsewhere, as in the low area near North Front and M streets, where water began to seep into basements that had never had water before. There was speculation about the possible relevance of the slurry pumping to this phenomenon. Meanwhile work continued in the downtown area and along the tracks with the grouting method.

By the time the city was fully involved in the subsidence problem, Keith West was deeply concerned with a personal matter. His first four-year term as mayor was marked by a shakeup and expansion of the police department under a new police chief, Russ Hawk, brought in from Douglas, Wyoming. West was reelected in 1982.

In September 1984 agents of the Federal Bureau of Investigation appeared at the headquarters of West's Desert Oil Company, north of Rock Springs, with an order from the federal court in Cheyenne authorizing them to seize many of the company's records. An affidavit filed at the court accused Desert

Oil of "shorting" customers—delivering fewer gallons of gasoline or diesel fuel than charged for. About eight months later, May 29, 1985, West appeared in the federal court to plead to charges filed against his company.

West, who had won election as "reform" and "clean up the town" candidate for mayor in 1978, had agreed to a plea bargain. The Desert Oil Company would be charged, but West as an individual would not be; West, as president of Desert Oil, would plead his company guilty to ten charges of shorting, and the U.S. attorney for the Wyoming district would forget about any other possible similar activities.

During the hearing Judge Clarence A. Brimmer asked, "I take it there are other counts that could be filed?"

The government attorney replied, "That's correct, Your Honor."

The judge: "How many?"

Attorney: "It depends on how we could approach this, Your Honor. It may be as many as several hundreds."

The judge read aloud in succession each of the ten different charges in the information and ten times the judge asked: "To this charge how does it [meaning the Desert Oil Company] plead?"

Ten times West answered: "Guilty."

Later in the hearing the judge asked West: "When you say the company did this, of course it didn't, but did you?"

West: "Under my direction."

The judge: "You did this? It isn't some employee that did it without your knowledge?"

West: "No, sir, under my direction."

The judge: "Yeah, you knew it was going on and you directed it to happen?"

West: "Yes, sir."

Desert Oil Company was fined $100,000 and ordered to make restitution of $75,000 to the customers involved in the charges.

At a city council meeting in Rock Springs following this court hearing West rejected a suggestion that he resign as mayor, and he was praised by at least five persons present at the meeting, including some members of the council. One person said she did not believe West's own statement that he knew about and directed the fraud. That was greeted by applause. West said he would continue as mayor. More applause.

Later, letters to law enforcement officers from Robert H. Johnson, Rock Springs attorney and former state senator, and from Wyoming District Judge Kenneth Hamm prompted further investigations under state laws into the activities of Desert Oil Company. This was apparently the principal reason for West's announcement that he would not run for reelection because of what he called the "crappy" nature of Rock Springs politics where his adversaries "keep up their book of dirty tricks."

Nobody ever said it was easy to live in Rock Springs, let alone try to be mayor.

Booms could come again. There are still between twelve and fifteen billion tons of coal underneath Sweetwater County, which is twice the size of Connecticut; and about two-thirds of that coal is high-grade bituminous concentrated in the Rock Springs uplift. The list of other resources that can be the basis of future prosperous times include: a trillion cubic feet of natural gas, three hundred million tons of trona, billions of tons of oil shale, deposits of uranium, and two billion tons of leucite. The leucite hills near Superior are the result of ancient lava flows and contain millions of tons of potash and alumina. Potash is used in fertilizers and has other uses; alumina (aluminum oxide) is used in making abrasives (emery). In addition, someday the sand dunes in northern Sweetwater County may be of value; the white sand could be valuable in making glass.

So good times and bad times will probably be coming again to Bitter Creek, where longtime residents still look puzzled when you ask why they stay there. They don't often wonder about that because for many of them moving away is not something they have seriously considered. A native of Rock Springs, Joe Fedrizzi, another son of Tyrolean parents, had opportunity to see other lands and other towns as an aviator during World War II. But he, like so many other war veterans, came back to Rock Springs. Why?

"Because I can walk down the street and say hello to just about everyone I meet, using first names," Joe said. "I call the president of my bank by his first name."

One bank president hundreds call by his first name is John Hay, Jr., who was still active in 1986 as president of the Rock Springs National, where he succeeded his father. His tall figure, still firmly straight and erect has been a familiar sight for years, striding up B Street on the way home for lunch. He and his brother, Leonard, who spends most of his time running the family ranch, are leading citizens, but if that notion of exalted status has occurred to them there is no hint of it in their relations with their fellow citizens. They are as comfortable as anyone with the first-name (or nickname) habit in Rock Springs.

Since the big boom one hears complaints that most of the people at the new shopping centers are strangers, but the long-time residents still believe a friendly community exists in their town. They keep at bay the sense of drab desolation visitors complain about with this friendly sharing that makes their lives cozy despite the harsh environment. Many private histories are still public knowledge among the long-timers. The genuine Rock Springsite is an expert "kinologist." Pronounce a name of a long-time resident and these people can recite next of kin, marriages, deaths, line of work, and future prospects. Rock Springs people practice this art almost every time they get together—"You remember . . ." someone will say, and then it rolls. It's not just gossip in Rock Springs; it's keeping the fabric of the community knitted, sort of a verbal photo album that they browse through with genuine affection. Two of the experts at "kinology" were two members of the *Rocket-Miner* news staff for years: Martha Jensen and Jessie Murphy.

There are more patches of lawn in Rock Springs now, more trees, more parks, impressive efforts to bring softening greenness to the city. Traffic clogged streets became a bad memory after the interstate highway was finished through the north section of town and a fine South Beltway constructed that swoops like a rollercoaster around the houses on the hills at the south edge. Also, newcomers have less cause for complaint about the lack of things to do. In addition to the golf course north of town and the recreation center created from a remodeled and expanded U.P. Old

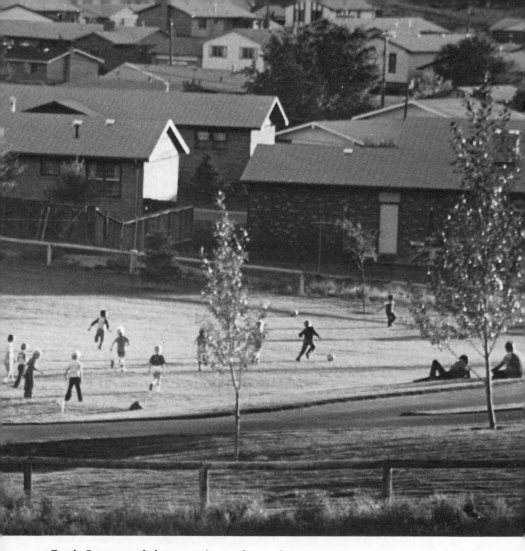

Rock Springs of the postenergy boom has a greener look, more grass, more trees, the result of planned effort. Grass in the parks is no longer dotted with Keep Off signs. A later afternoon game on the grass at Garnet Park in Prairie addition. *Photo by Author.*

Timers Building near where Chinatown used to be, Rock Springs in 1986 had opened another $10 million family recreation center and was building a new library, both at the west end. When the next boom comes—and if history tells us anything, it will—Rock Springs will be ready.

204

Even so, the look and mood of the desert still dominates, with buttes hovering above the town and a sandy presence that still comes right up to most front doors. And children still climb into the hills for roaming, sledding, exploring, and learning to deal with the open spaces.

There is an imperturability about the people of Rock Springs that is steadying. They have learned to live with the harshness around them. It's a healthy climate, if you respect it and are cautious. Take warm clothing and other survival gear in your car—always, even if driving on the interstate freeway. This is country that does not always give a second chance to the foolish or the unwary. Interstate 80 at one point literally follows the Continental Divide from which this land is suspended. It's about the same as being on the top of a 7,000-foot peak, except that on a peak you'd probably have a chance to scramble down to some sort of rocky, natural shelter in case of a storm. On the Red Desert shelter is nearly nonexistent, as three teenagers from Rock Springs learned on a holiday excursion. They wandered away from their car, lost their way in a sudden storm, and died out there.

Nevertheless, in and around Rock Springs at the time of sunset or sunrise the heavens declare His glory as they do everywhere else. When the desert is covered with snow that has been blown off the faces of the buttes and piled up behind any projection, even the tufts of sagebrush and greasewood, the shadows show soft tints of pastel colors as the sun drops toward the horizon. There will be streaks of orange, red, and yellow between the layers of gray clouds above the ragged line of buttes in the west. Watch closely and you may see brief tones of purple. You'll be looking at another reason why people stay in Rock Springs.

And maybe there's at least one other reason. Other towns in Wyoming, like Cheyenne, Laramie, and Sheridan, assumed an aura of stability and urbanity. Rock Springs never has. It still has an aura of the western frontier. To live on the banks of the Bitter Creek still takes grit.

Bibliography

Books

Adams, Henry H., *Years of Expectation, Guadalcanal to Normandy*, 1973

Allen, Fredrick Lewis, *Only Yesterday, An Informal History of the Nineteen Twenties*, 1931

Athearn, Robert G., *Union Pacific Country*, 1971

Barth, Gunther, *Bitter Strength, A History of the Chinese in the United States 1850-1870*, 1964

Bartlett, Richard A., *Great Surveys of the American West*, 1962

Beadle, J.H., *The Undeveloped West; or, Five Years in the Territories*, 1873

Bernstein, Irving, *Turbulent Years: A History of the American Worker 1933-1941*, 1970

Billington, Ray Allen, *Westward Expansion: A History of the American Frontier*, 1974

Bolognani, Bonifacio, *A Courageous People from the Dolomites*, published in Italy, 1981

Bowles, Samuel, *Across the Continent*, 1866

———, *Our New West*, 1869

Briggs, Harold E., *Frontiers of the Northwest*, 1950

(Bromley, Issac Hill), *The Chinese Massacre at Rock Springs, Wyoming Territory, Sept. 2, 1885*, 1886

Brown, Dee, *Hear that Lonesome Whistle Blow, Railroads in the West*, 1977

Coleman, McAlster, *Men and Coal*, 1943

Davis, John P., *The Union Pacific Railway*, 1894

Larson, T.A., *History of Wyoming*, 2nd ed., 1978

———, *Wyoming A Bicentennial History*, 1977

———, *Wyoming's War Years 1941-1945*, 1954

Lee, Calvin, *Chinatown, U.S.A.*, 1965

Lerner, Max, *America as a Civilization*, 1957

Lucia, Ellis, *The Saga of Ben Holladay*, 1959

McCague, James, *Moguls and Iron Men*, 1964

Mead, Jean, *Wyoming in Profile*, 1982

Murray, Robert A., *Military Posts of Wyoming*, 1974

Raine, William McLeod, and Will C. Barnes, *Cattle, Cowboys and Rangers*, 1930

Rickey, Jr., Don, *Forty Miles a Day on Beans and Hay*, 1963

Root, Frank A., and William E. Connelley, *The Overland Stage to California*, 1901 (reprinted 1950)

Roseberry, C.R., *The Challenging Skies—The Colorful Story of Aviation's Most Exciting Years 1919-1939*, 1966

Spence, Clark C., *The American West: A Source Book*

Spence, Gerry, *Gunning for Justice*

Stansbury, Howard, *An Expedition to the Valley of the Great Salt Lake of Utah . . . Also, a Reconnoissance of a New Route through the Rocky Mountains*, 1855

Stewart, Elinore Pruitt, *Letters of a Woman Homesteader*, 1914

Sung, Betty Lee, *Mountain of God. The Story of the Chinese in America*, 1967

Thernstrom, Stephan, editor, *Harvard Encyclopedia of American Ethnic Groups*, 1980

Time-Life, *The Soldier*, 1973

Trottman, Nelson, *History of the Union Pacific, A Financial and Economic Survey*, 1923

Urbanek, Mae, *Wyoming Wonderland*, 1964

Williamson, Jr., Chilton, *Roughnecking It*, 1982

Works Projects Administration, *Wyoming, A Guide to Its History, Highways, and People*, 1941

Wu, Cheng-Tsu, *"Chink!" A Documentary History of Anti-Chinese Prejudice in America*, 1972

Articles

Adams, Gerald M., "The Air Age Comes to Wyoming," *Annals of Wyoming*, Fall 1980, pp. 18-29

Arlen, Michael J., "The Air: The Prosecutor," *New Yorker*, November 28, 1977, pp. 166-173

Budd, Montgomery R., "The Union Pacific Coal Company, One of America's Great Mining Operations," *The Explosives Engineer*, May-June 1952, pp. 71-99

Chapman, Arthur, "The Sheep Herders of the West," *The Outlook*, June 24, 1905, pp. 481-488

Clarke, John Jackson, "Reminiscences of Wyoming in the Seventies and Eighties," *Annals of Wyoming*, July-October 1929, pp. 225-236

Coolidge, Susan, "A Few Hints on the California Journey," *Scribner's Monthly*, May 1873, pp. 25-31

Crane, Paul, and Alfred Larson, "The Chinese Massacre," *Annals of Wyoming*, January 1940, pp. 47-57, and April 1940, p. 153

Ehrlich, Gretel, "Wyoming, The Solace of Open Spaces," *The Atlantic*, May 1881, pp. 9-10

Friggens, Paul, "The Great Western Coal Rush," *Reader's Digest*, May 1974, pp. 104-108

Harger, Charles Moreau, "Sheep and Shepherds of the West," *The Outlook*, November 22, 1902, pp. 689-693

Krza, Paul, "King Coal in the Driver's Seat," *In Wyoming*, April-May 1976, p. 34

Murray, Robert A., "Fort Fred Steele: Desert Outpost on the Union Pacific," *Annals of Wyoming*, Fall 1972, pp. 193-206

Pryde, George B., "The Union Pacific Coal Company 1858 to August 1952," *Annals of Wyoming*, July 1953, pp. 191-205

"Rock Springs—Coming Up," *In Wyoming*, April-May 1976, pp. 43-50

(Richardson, Charles), "*Rocket-Miner* Grows Up with Rock Springs," *Rock Springs Rocket-Miner*, March 29, 1980, p. 10-A

Sargent, A.A., "The Wyoming Anti-Chinese Riot," *Overland Monthly*, November 1885, pp. 507-512

Shaw, Bill, "Hired Gun," *Chicago Tribune*, November 13, 1984, Section 5, p. 1

Sheils, Merrill, "Coal: Fuel of the Future," *Newsweek*, May 19, 1980, pp. 65-66

Snell, David, "The New Hunger for Coal Brings a Boom to Wyoming's Sweetwater County," *Smithsonian*, July 1974, pp. 73-79

Thayer, Mrs. D.M., "Story of the Growth of Rock Springs," *Rock Springs Miner*, September 7, 1917

Thomas, D.G., "How Rock Springs Celebrated Christmas in '78," *Annals of Wyoming*, April 1955, pp. 31-34

Van Zandt, Lt. J. Parker, U.S. Army Air Service, "On the Trail of the Air Mail," *National Geographic Magazine*, January 1926, pp. 1-61

Williamson, Jr., Chilton, "Jim Watt's Wyoming," *New Republic*, September 30, 1981, pp. 18-22

Newspapers and Magazines

Rock Springs Rocket Miner, Rock Springs, Wy.

Rock Springs Independent, Rock Springs, Wy.

Salt Lake Tribune, Salt Lake City, Ut.

The *Denver Post*, Denver, Co.

New York Times, New York, N.Y.

Laramie Boomerang, Laramie, Wy.

Casper Star-Tribune, Casper, Wy.

U.P. Coal Company, *Employee Magazine*, Rock Springs, Wy.

Pamphlets, Manuscripts, Documents

Bartholdi, Anita, "Melting Pot of Wyoming," unpublished manuscript, Rock Springs Public Library

Blackstone, Jr., D.L., *Traveler's Guide to the Geology of Wyoming*, 2nd ed., Laramie: Geological Survey of Wyoming, 1971

Chadey, Henry F., "The Chinese Story and Rock Springs, Wyoming," manuscript, Sweetwater County Historical Museum

Clark, Mary A., "Pioneer Days in Rock Springs 1881-1898," interview with Mrs. Dan Potter, Wyoming Archives

Complaint for Defamation, Paul Wataha v Columbia Broadcasting System, Inc., a New York corporation; Dan Rather; Paul L. Loewenwarter; William J. Luzmoor, III; Media West, Inc., a Wyoming corporation; Rock Springs Newspapers, Inc., a Wyoming corporation;

Charles C. Richardson; Margaret Richardson; Greg Messel; Timely, Inc., a Wyoming corporation; E.D. Stone; and Clyde Kemp. District Court of Sweetwater County, Wyoming, Third Judicial District, October 16, 1978

Cullen, Thomas P., "Rock Springs: Growing Up in a Wyoming Coal Town, 1915-1938," typewritten manuscript, 1985, Sweetwater County Historical Museum

Darling, Mrs. George, paper read at meeting of Woman's Club, published in *Rock Springs Miner*, February 15, 1924

Emery, Ezra L., Letterpress book 1900-06, Wyoming Archives

Fletcher, Erma A., "A History of the Labor Movement in Wyoming 1870-1940," M.A. thesis, University of Wyoming, 1945

Harmston, Floyd, *An Economic Study of Sweetwater County, Wyoming*, prepared for the Wyoming Industrial Research Council by Division of Economic Analysis, College of Commerce and Industry, University of Wyoming

"Incidents of Pioneer Days in Rock Springs," Wyoming Archives

"Industrial Review 1921," pamphlet published by *Rock Springs Rocket*

McAuliffe, Eugene, *Early Coal Mining in the West*, pamphlet published by the Newcomen Society of England, American Branch, New York, 1948

National Archives, microfilm publications, Microcopy No. 689, "Letters Received by the Office of Adjutant General," (Main Series) 1881-1889, Roll 386, 1885

National Archives, Returns from U.S. Military Posts, 1800-1916, Microfilm 978.02, microcopy 617, reel 926, Camp Pilot Butte, Wyoming, September 1885-February 1899

Outsen, Brig. Gen. Robert, "Rock Springs Massacre," typewritten manuscript, Wyoming Archives

Peterson, Henry J., "The Constitutional Convention of Wyoming," University of Wyoming Publications, Vol. III, No. 6, May 1, 1940

Schultz, A.R., "The Northern Part of the Rock Springs Coal Field, Sweetwater County, Wyoming," USGS Bulletin 341, Washington, 1909

———, "The Southern Part of the Rock Springs Coal Field, Sweetwater County, Wyoming," USGS Bulletin 381, 1910

———, "Oil Possibilities in and around Baxter Basin in the Rock Springs Uplift, Sweetwater County, Wyoming," USGS Bulletin 702,

Washington, 1920

Thomas, David G., "Chinese Riot," as told to his daughter, Mrs. J.H. Goodnough, typewritten manuscript, Sweetwater County Historical Museum

———, Letters to state historian, Wyoming Archives

Union Pacific Coal Company, "Some Facts Relative to the Oldest and Largest Producer of Coal in the Western United States," pamphlet published by the company in effort to attract "law-abiding workmen."

United States of America v Desert Oil Company, Transcript of Arraignment and Sentencing Proceedings, U.S. District Court, District of Wyoming, May 29, 1985

Wataha, Paul, "The Rock Springs, Wyoming, Experience," speech delivered before Utah Joint Legislative Committee on Energy Policy, August 10, 1976

Webb, Grace, "Rock Springs International Night," typewritten manuscript, Wyoming Archives

Wilde, Gisela (Bertagnolli), "My Memoirs," handwritten manuscript, Sweetwater County Historical Museum

Wilson, Arlen Ray, "The Rock Springs, Wyoming, Chinese Massacre," M.A. thesis, University of Wyoming, 1967

Yates, W., "Rock Springs When This Century Was Young," typewritten manuscript, Sweetwater County Museum

Yourston, R.E., "The Rock Springs Coal Field," Wyoming Geological Association Guidebook, Tenth Annual Field Conference, 1955

Index

Index